# Programming with MFC
# & Visual C++

## Electrical and Electronic Engineering Design Series
Electric Circuits Analysis and Design

Electronic Circuit Design   with Bipolar and MOS Transistors

CMOS Circuit Design Analog, Digital, IC Layout

Digital Design Logic, Memory, Computers

Analog Filter Design

Error Correction Code Design


## Computer Science Design Series
Programming with MFC & Visual C++


## Mathematics
Arithmetic – Integers, Fractions, Decimals

Algebra – A Clear Presentation

# Programming with MFC & Visual C++

Nicholas L. Pappas, Ph.D.

© 2017 Nicholas L. Pappas, Ph.D.

All Rights Reserved Worldwide.
Except as permitted under the Copyright Act of 1976, no part of this book may be reproduced in whole or in part in any manner. Not in any form or by any electronic or mechanical means, nor stored in a retrieval system, or, transmitted, in any form or by any means, electronic, mechanical, photocopying, recording, or otherwise, without the express permission of Nicholas L. Pappas, Ph.D.
ISBN 13: 978 1975 776 312      ISBN 10: 1975 776 313

---

**A Message about this Text:** The subject is essentially endless. The purpose here is to say enough about the subject so that you, the reader, have a running start when you apply this knowledge to your work.

Knowing how to program in C, C++, C# expedites programming with MFC. However, knowing very little about programming in C, C++, & C# we show how, *with significant effort,* one can get a good head start programming with MFC.

The required accessory to the text is Visual C++ (or later version). And, Jeff Prosise's text "Programming Windows with MFC" is, as a practical matter, a required yet optional accessory.

These efforts provide *startup* work experience. Once you have some work experience we are confident that you will be able to expand your know how with reasonable effort.

---

**A Message from the Author:** I have worked continuously in the electronics industry since 1950 except for 11 semesters teaching at San Jose State University (Professor and Chair Computer Engineering 1988-1993). There I discovered my talent for teaching such as it may be. After War2 I attended Lehigh University, and then transferred to Stanford where I earned the MS degree and, while working at HP in the early 1950's, the Ph.D. EE degree. (Somehow I did not get the word and formally apply for the BS degree.) Hardware design has been my principal activity. I learned enough about assembly language, Forth, C and C++ to design the software I needed for my projects. My current activity is designing integrated circuits.

# Preface

This is about how to use Windows MFC[1] and Visual C++[2] to write programs using windows without knowing how to write the complex code that produces the windows. The MFC/Visual C++ combination immensely simplifies the writing of any program that uses one or more windows.

However there is a catch. You have to discover the MFC functions that, for example, draw to the screen, do math, do file read and write, etc unless you are eager to write them. Finding the functions and learning how to use them is a time consuming process that is reduced significantly if you own a copy of Jeff Prosise's 1337 page text[3].

Nevertheless, we expect you to have a basic programming capability.

MFC classes and functions replace many C, C++, and C# classes and functions. Consequently even beginners with some programming experience can go directly to MFC, and save a lot of time and energy. Programming with MFC allows you to work at the top of the C hierarchy, while avoiding the limitations of C, C++, and C#.

This text only *begins* to show you how to program with MFC by using Visual C++ to produce skeleton programs on the Visual C++ screen. Skeletons that include code producing the windows in which your programs will be presented. You add your program code to the skeletons.

We say *begin*, because learning how to program in any language is an endless task.

There is an unavoidable "cook book" element to using Visual C++ that dictates how to create the skeletons, and where to enter your code in the skeletons.

This text is different. Instead of explanations that assume you "know" leaving you wondering what to do next, we assume you do not "know"

---

[1] Microsoft Foundation Classes
[2] A Microsoft software program also known as Visual Studio
[3] Jeff Prosise, "Programming Windows with MFC", Second Edition,. ISBN 1572 316 950 (an electronic copy is included in most Visual Studio products)

# Programming with MFC

as we show you how to add code to the MFC skeleton that actually creates programs that run on any computer using the windows operating system.

Most of the time, JP's text tells us what functions to use. The MFC library, included with Visual C++, tells us how to use them (sometimes – nothing is perfect here). And then, there is the F1 key (see below).

Once a skeleton program is created [JP213] [4], the next problem, as mentioned above, surfaced. We know we want functions to do such and such, but do they exist in MFC or do we have to create them? As will become clear later some do exist, and some we had to write in order to implement *message handlers*.

With Jeff Prosise's text supporting us we were able to find functions that enabled us to write programs using windows, while knowing nothing about windows programming and very little about MFC and the various C languages. JP's text gave us a great start with the design process producing programs presented in one or more windows.

That experience brings us to this point. We wrote this text, because even with the JP reference we learned that we had to answer many "How-do-we-do-that?" questions. Answers we needed in order to produce programs that run. Answers we share with you by presenting selected topics in the form of working projects.

Many types of programs can be implemented with MFC. We focus on dot exe (name.exe) executing programs.

**Visual C++ is very unforgiving. Certain types of errors cannot be corrected (or we do not know how to correct). You have to delete the workspace (program) folder and start over. This usually happens when errors are made using Class Wizard. This is one reason why you would be wise to write down what you do as you proceed. Write a narrative such as that in any one of the chapters in our text.**

> JP's text makes very clear the fact that there is much, much more to MFC then what we present here.

> We use Visual C++ 6.0

---

[4] [JP213] means go to page 213 of JP's text.

# Preface

As you read our text it is necessary that the Microsoft Visual C++ program is up and running. We strongly recommend that JP's text is right there next to you.

*Emphasis*: The Visual C++ program, supported by the MFC, immensely facilitates (windows) program design.

**A Note about Compilation errors** When errors occur while building (compiling) a program in Visual C++ the reasons why appear in the output pane of the Visual C++ screen display. The reasons why may be numerous and many appear to be weird. This can happen when a merely a semicolon is omitted at the end of a statement.

Therefore, do what we do, always build and run a program to check for errors EVERY TIME YOU ADD A CODE LINE so that you know where to look.

We have never had to use the debug facility by building every time we added one or more lines simply because the error(s) had to be in the small number of line(s) we just added.

> All of the code in this book is protected by copyright.
> Using our programs for commercial gain is a no-no.

*IMPORTANT- the F1 key: Visual C++ simplifies finding information via the F1 key. For example, anywhere in the Visual C++ right hand screen where the code appears, type any word, highlight it, and press F1. If the word is not legal it simply appears in the index edit box. If the word is legal the MSDN library Topics Found dialog box appears. Click on the line in the box that selects the Microsoft Foundation Class library function.*

> Our blog *npappasee.blogspot.com* may offer you additional information. Take a look.

> We would appreciate receiving your comments and views on this text at *npappasz@yahoo.com*.

Programming with MFC

# Contents

## 1 How Visual C++ Works ............................................................................ 1
1.1 Single document/view ............................................................................. 2
1.2 Multiple document/view .......................................................................... 3
1.3 Dialog based ............................................................................................ 4
1.4 Build and Execute a project .................................................................... 4
1.5 Writing the Window's Title .................................................................... 5

## 2 Hello World Program Design ................................................................... 6

## 3 Drawing in a Window ............................................................................... 7

## 4 Signal Generator Front Panel Project .................................................. 11
4.1 Create a Project Workspace ................................................................. 12
4.2 Build the Signal Generator Project ...................................................... 12
4.3 Change Dialog size and delete controls. .............................................. 12
4.4 How to Position a Control .................................................................... 14
4.5 Keypad and Code for Programming a Number ................................... 16
    4.5.1 Add a Push Button, Position it, Change Properties ..................... 16
    4.5.2 Add Push Button Handlers for Message Passing ........................ 18
    4.5.3 Add Code to Keypad Skeleton Push Button Message Handlers ... 20
    4.5.4 Add Push Button Member Variables ............................................ 25
    4.5.5 Add *OnPaint* Code ....................................................................... 26
4.6 Code for Programming a Frequency .................................................... 27
4.7 Code for Programming a Waveform .................................................... 32
4.8 Functions that support the Waveform Display .................................... 37
4.9 A Simple Help Program ........................................................................ 42
4.10 Summary: Variables, Initialize Variables .......................................... 43

## 5 Oscilloscope Front Panel Dialog Project .............................................. 45
5.1 Create a Project Workspace ................................................................. 46
5.2 Build the Oscilloscope Project .............................................................. 46
5.3 Change Dialog size and delete OK and Cancel Buttons. .................... 46
5.4 Code for Adding a Push Button ........................................................... 49
5.5 Code for Adding a Combo Box ............................................................. 54
5.6 Code for Adding a Slider ...................................................................... 58
5.7 Code for Combo Box and Slider Variables ......................................... 63
5.8 Code for Support Functions .................................................................. 64
5.9 A Simple Help Program ........................................................................ 66

# Contents

## 6 Design a Property Sheet connected to a Menu Button ............ 67
6.1 Create the *PropSheetMenu* Workspace ..................................................... 67
6.2 Build the *PropSheetMenu* Project and Change Title ............................... 67
6.3 Use *ResourceView* to create four Property Page Dialog Boxes............... 68
6.4 Use *ClassWizard* to create four pairs of Property Page Files .................. 69
6.5 Use *ClassWizard* to create a Property Sheet............................................. 70
6.6 Add Controls to the Property Pages........................................................... 71
      6.6.1 Selecting Rectangle Color (CPage2)............................................ 72
      6.6.2 Selecting Rectangle Size (CPage1)............................................. 74
6.7 PropSheet Menu Button Opens Property Sheet......................................... 76
6.8 The Apply Button Transfers the Data........................................................ 78
6.9 Displaying a Rectangle on the Screen ....................................................... 79

## 7 More About Sliders ..................................................................... 80
8.1 Create a Dialog Based Project Workspace ................................................ 80
8.2 Build the *Slider* Project............................................................................. 80
8.3 Add Controls to Slider Example Dialog Box ............................................ 82

## 8 Tic Tac Toe – a Document/View Project ................................... 85
8.1 Create the *TicTacToe* project Workspace ................................................. 86
8.2 Build and Execute the *TicTacToe* Project................................................. 86
8.3 Code for Document Functions .................................................................... 86
8.4 Code for View Functions............................................................................. 92
      8.4.1 Code for Drawing on the Screen .................................................. 93
      8.4.2 Code for Mouse Events and Message Handlers.......................... 96
8.5 Code for Menu Items .................................................................................. 98

## 9 ADD - a Project........................................................................... 101
9.1 Preparing *OnDraw* and *OnChar*............................................................. 107
9.2 The Caret and the Font ............................................................................. 109
9.3 Setting Up the Problem ............................................................................ 112
9.4 Displaying the Problem ............................................................................ 116
9.5 Creating the Numbers to Add................................................................... 118
9.6 A Key Press Skeleton ............................................................................... 120
9.7 Processing Setup-the-Problem Key Presses ............................................ 121
9.8 How the User Solves the Problem............................................................ 125
9.9 Processing Do-The-Problem Key Presses ............................................... 127
9.10 What-to-do-next Message Handlers....................................................... 132
9.11 A Simple Help Function......................................................................... 134
9.12 Variable Definitions and Initial Values ................................................. 135

## Index ................................................................................................ 136

# 1 How Visual C++ Works

Visual C++ creates a project workspace (a folder) that contains the set of code files that define the *code skeleton* of a project. The set of files is a working skeleton to which you add code to create a functioning project. Here is how Visual C++ 6.0 works.

Two wizards, AppWizard and ClassWizard, are the Visual C++ code generators. AppWizard creates the working skeleton code of a Windows project with features you can specify via dialog boxes (resources) inserted into the project. When creating workspaces we make choices of the available options. Your choices may be different given the needs of your project.

ClassWizard facilitates adding new classes, new variables, as well as assist you in other code writing procedures. ClassWizard is used and explained in later chapters where projects are implemented.

The focus here is on creating executable files with the dot exe extension. There are three types of dot exe projects to choose from. We show how to create one of each in what follows.

**An Unnecessary Problem** There are unnecessary trivial differences amongst the various versions of Visual C++. The differences make the project creation processes *appear* to be different when they in fact they have the same goal - to create projects. The Visual C++ 6.0 processes are presented below. In your version look for the same words, which are found in various contexts. OK – here we go.

**First** create a folder in your directory in which your project workspace folders will be stored. We named the folder *Project X*.

**Second** open Visual C++ to get a Window containing three empty panes, tool bars and a status bar. The third pane, the output pane, may not present. To see the output pane click on *View*, click on *Output*.

Programming with MFC

1 Click *File* menu. Click *New* to get the *New* dialog box [JP213], which has 4 tabs. Select the *Projects* page tab. The page contains a list of project types you can create. Highlight *MfcAppWizard(exe)*. (Executing files, dot exe files, are produced by *MfcAppWizard(exe).* )

2 *Choose Directory* In the *Projects* page (of the *New* dialog box) click on the small "box" to the right of the *Location* edit box.

This opens the *Choose Directory* dialog box. In the *Drives* box select the drive that stores *Project X*. In the *Directory name* box select the folder *Project X* that you want to store your project folders in. Click on *OK* to exit the *Choose Directory* dialog box, and return to *New*.

In the *Project name* edit box (of the *New* dialog box) type the project name *Learn* (or whatever name you want). Note the addition of *Learn* to the path in the *Location* edit box. Observe that *Create new workspace* has been selected, and that the *Platform* is Win32.

Click OK. This opens the AppWizard *Step 1* screen. You have 3 choices – single document (1.1), multiple document (1.2), and dialog (1.3)

The *Learn* folder has been created. Take a look in folder *Project X*. From here on you are using AppWizard

## 1.1 Single document/view

01) In the *MFC AppWizard - Step 1* screen - select *Single document*, select *Document/View architecture support*, and select your language. Click Next.

02) In the *MFC AppWizard - Step 2 of 6* screen select *none*. Database support not required. Click Next.

03) In the *MFC AppWizard - Step 3 of 6* screen uncheck *ActiveX Controls*. Select *none*. Compound document support not required. Click Next.

04) In the *MFC AppWizard - Step 4 of 6* screen select only *Docking toolbar* and *Initial status bar*. Select *Normal* toolbar look. Click Next.

05) In the *MFC AppWizard - Step 5 of 6* screen select *MFC Standard*. Click Next.

# 1 How Visual C++ Works

06) In the *MFC AppWizard - Step 6 of 6* screen click Finish.

07) In the *New Project Information* dialog box click *OK* to enter the *Learn* workspace.

You are done - the *Learn* workspace has been created on screen. In the left pane you can examine the project classes, resources, and files. Go to Section 1.4. When you are done *Click File* menu, click *Close Workspace*.

## 1.2 Multiple document/view

11) In the *MFC AppWizard - Step 1* screen - select *Multiple documents*, accept *Document/View architecture support*, and select your language. Click Next.

12) In the *MFC AppWizard - Step 2 of 6* screen select *none*. Database support not required. Click Next.

13) In the *MFC AppWizard - Step 3 of 6* screen uncheck *ActiveX Controls*. Select *none*. Compound document support not required. Click Next.

14) In the *MFC AppWizard - Step 4 of 6* screen select only *Docking toolbar* and *Initial status bar*. Select *Normal* toolbar look. Click Next.

15) In the *MFC AppWizard - Step 5 of 6* screen select *MFC Standard*. Click Next.

16) In the *MFC AppWizard - Step 6 of 6* screen click Finish.

17) In the *New Project Information* dialog box click *OK* to enter the *Learn* workspace.

You are done - the *Learn* workspace has been created on screen. In the left pane you can examine the project classes, resources, and files. Go to Section 1.4. When you are done *Click File* menu, click *Close Workspace*.

Programming with MFC

## 1.3 Dialog based

Do Single document/view steps 1 and 2 to create project *Dialog*.
21) In the *MFC AppWizard - Step 1* screen select *Dialog based*, select your language. Click Next.

22) In the *MFC AppWizard - Step 2 of 4* screen uncheck 3 boxes – *about, 3D Controls, ActiveX controls.* You can type your title of the dialog box or accept what is written. Click Next.

23) In the *MFC AppWizard - Step 3 of 4* screen select *MFC Standard* Click Next.

24) In the *MFC AppWizard – Step4 of 4* screen click Finish.

25) In the *New Project Information* dialog box click *OK* to enter the *Dialog* workspace.

You are done - the *Dialog* workspace has been created on screen. In the left pane you can examine the project classes, resources, and files. Go to Section 1.4. When you are done *Click File* menu, click *Close Workspace*.

## 1.4 Build and Execute a project

Building a project is straightforward. Build to verify that the project workspace is error free. Watch the build progress in the output pane

To build the project click on *Build menu.*
Click on *Set Active Configuration*
    In the *Set Active Configuration* dialog box click on
    *Learn - Win32Release*, click on OK.
Then
Click on *Build menu.*
Click on *Build Project-name.exe*. Watch the output pane. You should see *Learn.exe - 0 error(s), 0 warning(s)*.
Click on *Build menu.*
Click on *Execute Project-name.exe*
*Learn* Window appears. The window is empty. The window title is "Untitled – Learn."

1 How Visual C++ Works

> Later - After adding code to any project file repeat Build a Project to check for errors.

Examine the files: At the bottom of the left hand panel on the screen click on FileView. In FileView click on all titles until all file names are exposed. Click on a file name. Examine the file contents in the right hand screen panel.

**Important:** execute a program after a build to make sure it works.
**A quick way to open any workspace**
For example open the *Learn* workspace folder in the Project X folder. Click on *Learn.dsw*. Right click on *Learn.dsw*. Click on *Open with MSDEV*. This action opens Visual C++ and the *Learn* workspace.

**Where is the dot exe file?**
Open the Learn workspace folder. Dot exe is in the release folder.

## 1.5 Writing the Window's Title

Writing your title in a window title bar is simply a matter of modifying a string. Open the *Learn* workspace.

In the *ResourceView* pane click on *Learn resources*, click on *String Table*, click on *String Table*.

In the right hand pane click on the IDR_MAINFRAME string. Right click on the string and select properties. Change the strings' **bold type** as shown below. Simply exchange **Learn** and **\n**.

From
**Learn\n\n**Learn\n\n\nLearn.Document\nLearn Document
To
**\nLearn\n**Learn\n\n\nLearn.Document\nLearn Document
Click on X.

Build the project, the execute it. The window title is now Learn.

> If you do not like what has been done in a project you can delete it. Exit Visual C++. Go to the Project X folder. Delete the project folder.

# 2 Hello World Program Design

The traditional "first program" writes the message "Hello World" in a window.

Open Visual C++. Create a single document workspace with name *HelloWorld* (Chapter 1, Section 1.1). Click on *FileView* in the left pane. Click on the source file *HelloWorldView.cpp*. The contents of *HelloWorldView.cpp* appear on the screen.

Since everything in the client window is *drawn* we look for a text drawing function to add to *OnDraw*. We find *TextOut* in the Drawing Text section [JP67].

BOOL TextOut( int *x*, int *y*, const CString& *str* );

The parameter *str* is written as _T ("Hello World"). The MFC _T macro [JP32] used here makes a program indifferent to character set differences. The macro is used as _T (string in quotes).

The *pDC* –> *TextOut* line is the only code line added (by hand) to *OnDraw* in *HelloWorldView.cpp*. The arrow operator is used to call *TextOut*, because the *OnDraw* argument *pDC* is a pointer.

---

```
void CHelloWorldView::OnDraw(CDC* pDC)
{
    CHelloWorldDoc* pDoc = GetDocument();
    ASSERT_VALID(pDoc);
    // TODO: add draw code for native data here
    pDC -> TextOut (200, 200, _T("Hello World") );
}
```

---

Click on *Build*. (Chapter 1, Section 1.4).
Click on *Build HelloWorld.exe*.
Click on *Execute HelloWorld.exe*
Take a look. Compare this to JP16.

Change 200, 200 to any other x, y coordinates to move the text in the window.

# 3 Drawing in a Window

Windows graphics programming was simplified when the *CDC* Graphics Device Interface (GDI) appeared, because the GDI is a *device independent* graphics interface. Furthermore MFC adds MFC classes and functions that enhance and work with the GDI. [JP37 – Chapter 2]

There are two functions that draw in a window: *OnPaint* and *OnDraw*. The document/view architecture (Chapter 9) uses *OnDraw* [JP504]. *OnPaint* [JP27] is used by *non* document/view architectures such as dialog. The functions are called by the WM_PAINT message.

**Device context** Windows drawing functions draw in the device context's logical display surface instead of screen pixels. The GDI uses the device context idea [JP38] to ensure that every program draws in its own window, and does not interfere with any other program window,

Before a Windows program can draw any pixels on the screen it must acquire a device context handle from the GDI before being able to draw.

There are four MFC Special Purpose Device Context Classes [JP39].
Class Name  Description
*CPaintDC*     For drawing in a window's client area by message handlers
*CClientDC*    For drawing in a window's client area anywhere *OnPaint* does not draw
*CWindowDC*    For drawing anywhere in a window
*CMetaFileDC*  For drawing to a GDI metafile

Using a device context is straightforward in *OnPaint( )* for example:

```
void CSignalGenDlg::OnPaint()
{
    CPaintDC dc(this);      // device context for painting
    // rectangle definition
    int x1 = 37, dx1 = 80;
    int y1 = 60, dy1 = 20;
    dc.Rectangle (x1, y1, x1+dx1, y1+dy1);   // the body of the rectangle
    CString m_strNumber = _T("1234567");
    dc.TextOut (x1+10, y1+1, m_strNumber);   // print the Number}
```

Programming with MFC

**Device Context Attributes** A device context has many attributes [JP42] such as text color, background color, mapping mode, drawing mode, and current position.

**The Drawing Mode** When the GDI sends pixels to the logical display surface the pixel colors are combined with the pixel colors at the destination by a Boolean operation [JP44].

**The Mapping Mode** Logical coordinates are passed to the output. A mapping mode converts the logical coordinates into device coordinates. [JP45]. There are 8 GDI mapping modes [JP46].

**Coordinate Conversions** The *CDC::LPtoDP* function converts logical coordinates to device coordinates. And, *CDC::DPtoLP* function converts device coordinates to logical coordinates [JP49].

**Moving the Origin** The default device context origin is the upper left window corner. MFC's *CDC* class includes two functions that move the origin. *CDC::SetWindowOrg* moves the window origin. The viewport origin is moved by *CDC::SetviewportOrg* [JP50].

Drawing with the GDI

**Objects that Draw** The classes *CPen*, *CBrush*, and *CFont* define pens, brushes, and fonts [JP 60, 64, 69].

The default pen draws solid black lines 1 pixel wide. The default brush paints areas solid white. The default font is a proportional font with a 12 point height.

```
// Here is how to create your pen [JP60].
CPen name ( int nPenStyle, int nWidth, COLORREF crColor );
// For example create a CPen object myredpen and define it
CPen myredpen (PS_SOLID, 4, RGB (255, 0, 0) ;
// or
BOOL CreatePen ( int nPenStyle, int nWidth, COLORREF crColor);
// For example
CPen mybluepen;       // creates CPen object mybluepen.
mybluepen.CreatPen (PS_SOLID, 10, RGB(0, 0, 255);   //use the dot operator
```

# 3 Drawing in a Window

// Brushes can be solid, hatched, or patterned.
// Here is how to create your solid brush [JP64].
**CBrush** name **( COLORREF** *crColor* **);**
// For example
CBrush yellow_brush (RGB(255,255,100));

//or
**BOOL CreateSolidBrush (COLORREF** *crColor* **);**
// For example
CBrush yellow_brush;          // create CBrush object yellow_brush
yellow_brush.CreateSolidBrush (RGB(255,255,100));

---

//Here is how to create your hatched brush [JP65].
**CBrush** name (int *nIndex*, **COLORREF** *crColor*);
CBrush blue_brush (HS_CROSS, RGB (0, 0, 255));   //for example
  /* **Parameters**
  *nIndex* Specifies the hatch style of the brush. It can be any one of several styles [JP65]
  *crColor* Specifies the foreground color of the brush as an RGB color. If the brush is hatched, this parameter specifies the color of the hatching.   */

---

**Basic code for drawing:** Draw using pDC –> object [JP39].

   CDC * pDC = GetDC ();          // Get Device Context
   // Do some drawing
   ReleaseDC (pDC);

**Changing an Object** *CDC::SelectObject* is the *CDC* function used to select a predefined GDI object into a device context. *SelectObject* selects predefined Pens, Brushes, Fonts, Bitmaps, and other objects into a device context [JP73]. Emphasis: Until *SelectObject* is used to change the current pen, brush, or font, the GDI uses the device context's defaults.

ACTION Create a single document workspace with name *Drawing*. (Chapter 1, Sections 1.1, 1.4, 1.5). Click on *FileView* in the left pane. Click on the source file *DrawingView.cpp*. The contents of *DrawingView.cpp* appear on the screen. After adding Code 301 page 10 build the program (Ch 1, Section 1.4).

Programming with MFC

**Code 301 Add this sample of drawing code to *OnDraw* in *DrawingView.cpp***

```cpp
void CDrawingView::OnDraw(CDC* pDC)
{
    CDrawingDoc* pDoc = GetDocument();      // already there – do not copy
    ASSERT_VALID(pDoc);                      // already there – do not copy
    // Draw using pDC -> object
    pDC = GetDC ();            // Get Device Context

    // TODO: Add your message handler code here
    pDC -> SetMapMode (MM_LOENGLISH);
    pDC -> MoveTo (100,-20);
    pDC -> LineTo (500, -20);

    //Pen functions
    CPen redpen (PS_SOLID,4,RGB(255,0,0));
    CPen* pOldPen = pDC -> SelectObject (&redpen);
    pDC -> LineTo (100,-60);

    CPen bluepen (PS_SOLID,10,RGB(0,0,255));
    CPen* pOldPen1 = pDC -> SelectObject (&bluepen);
    pDC -> LineTo (500,-60);

    pDC -> SelectObject (pOldPen);
    pDC -> MoveTo (100,-100);
    pDC -> LineTo (500,-100);
    //Brush and pen functions
    CBrush blue_brush(HS_CROSS, RGB(0,0,255));
    pDC -> SelectObject (&blue_brush);
    CPen* pOldPen2 = pDC -> SelectObject (&redpen);
    pDC -> Rectangle (100, -80, 500, -140);
    CBrush yellow_brush(RGB(255,255,100));
    pDC -> SelectObject (&yellow_brush);
    CPen* pOldPen3 = pDC -> SelectObject (&redpen);
    CRect rect(100, -180, 500, -240);

    pDC -> Rectangle (100, -180, 500, -240);
    pDC -> SetBkMode (TRANSPARENT);
    pDC -> DrawText (_T ("Write in a box"),-1, &rect, DT_SINGLELINE |
                                    DT_CENTER | DT_VCENTER);
    pDC -> Ellipse (100, -260, 500, -320);
    pDC -> RoundRect (100, -360, 500, -420, 20, 20);
    ReleaseDC (pDC);
}
```

# 4 Signal Generator Front Panel Project

A Signal Generator Design project is a working design with three parts: 1) the Signal Generator front panel on the PC screen, 2) the Universal Serial Bus channel, and 3) the Signal Generator hardware that produces signals defined by the front panel via the USB bus. What follows is only about the Signal Generator front panel on the PC screen, because this is about how to program a *dialog based* project using Visual C++.

Knowing that everything on the front panel *has to be drawn* is the key to understanding how a front panel is created.

After opening a *dialog based* project workspace the *front panel* is created in the form of a dialog box *as a main window* [JP432], which is resized to the design size. Then control push buttons and radio buttons are added at locations established by the design. Text boxes showing the current numbers for parameters are added next to associated control buttons. Text labels identify groups of control functions.

The event driven Windows programming model means that clicking on a control is an event that sends a message that calls a message handler function that implements the control's purpose. This capability is implemented by adding MFC skeleton code for event driven message passing. At this point the message handler functions are empty. Each message handler function is then written in MFC code according to the needs of the design. Finally required functions are written to support the message handlers. This completes the front panel design.

The design works as follows. First you *Enter a Number* (Figure 401). The number is entered via the 0 to 9 keypad. If the number is intended to be the *Begin* frequency of a sweep, then you click the *Begin* push button.

Pressing any push button such as *Begin* produces two actions.
1) The number is stored in a register and displayed on the front panel.
2) The number is sent, via the USB bus, to program the hardware.

After all parameters required to program the Signal Generator have been entered press *Start* to produce the signal. Press *Stop* when you are done.

Programming with MFC

## 4.1 Create a dialog based project workspace.

Follow the procedure in Chapter 1, Section 1.3 Dialog Based except as follows.
    Type the name *SignalGen* in the *Project Name* edit box.
    Note addition of *SignalGen* in the *Location* edit box.
    In step 2 of 4 screen type the title *Signal Generator 1Hz to 50MHz*

## 4.2 Build the *SignalGen* Project

Follow the procedure in Chapter 1, Section 1.4.

## 4.3 Change Dialog size and delete controls

Click on *File*, click on *Open* to get the *Open* dialog box
Change contents of the *Open as* edit box to *Text*
Click on *SignalGen.rc*
Click on Open to open the *dot rc* file
Go to the file's *Dialog* section, and change from
IDD_SIGNALGEN_DIALOG DIALOGEX 0, 0, 320, 200
to
IDD_SIGNALGEN_DIALOG DIALOGEX 0, 0, 600, 200

Click on File, click on *Save as* to get *Save as* dialog box, click on *Save*.
Close the *SignalGen.rc* file.

Click *ResourceView* at bottom of left pane.
Click on +SignalGen Resources.
Click on +Dialog.
Click on IDD_SIGNALGEN_DIALOG.
Observe the new size of the dialog box (the front panel to be).

Click on the *OK* button. Right click, select cut to remove button
(You may want to retain the OK button and use it as an exit button)
Click on the *Cancel* button. Right click, select cut to remove button
Click on *text*. Right click, select cut to remove the text.

> Emphasis: The dialog box is the front panel

# 4 Signal Generator Front Panel Project

**Figure 401 Signal Generator Front Panel Design**

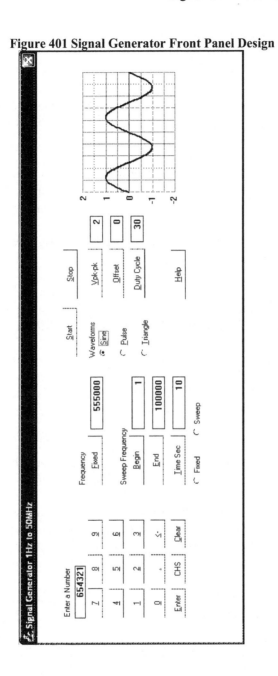

Programming with MFC

## 4.4 How to Position a Control

Positioning is *complicated* in Visual C++.

To display the front panel click ResourceView, +SignalGen Resources, +Dialog, and IDD_SIGNALGEN_DIALOG. Click on the front panel to put the focus on it.

There is a status bar directly below the front panel. Click on the square of dots (Toggle Grid) next to the right end of the status bar. A dot grid appears on the front panel. Click again and the dots disappear.

Next, click on the funny square (Toggle Guides) at the right end. Then toggle between *Rulers & Guides* and a plain panel display. End toggling on *Rulers & Guides*.

You can achieve the same results of you click on *Layout* in the tool bar, click on guide Settings, and then any of the 3 *Layout Guides*. Do not change the *Grid Spacing*.

When in the *Rulers & Guides* display, place the cursor on a ruler and click. Observe that an arrow and a gridline appear. Put the cursor over the arrow, or the gridline, and a ↔ symbol appears. Press and hold the left mouse button, observe that dimensions appear.

Place the cursor on the ruler. Press and release the right mouse button. A box appears. Click on clear to remove the grid line.

The arrows and grid lines allow exact positioning. For example do this: on the x axis place the cursor at coordinates 25, 60, and 95 to get gridlines at coordinates 25, 60, and 95. Repeat for the y axis at coordinates 50, 70, 90, 110, and 130 (Figure 404).

>>> The arrow keys on the keyboard move selected objects, such as buttons, in small increments.

Retain the gridlines forever. They simplify the positioning task.

# 4 Signal Generator Front Panel Project

**Figure 404 Signal Generator Control Grid**

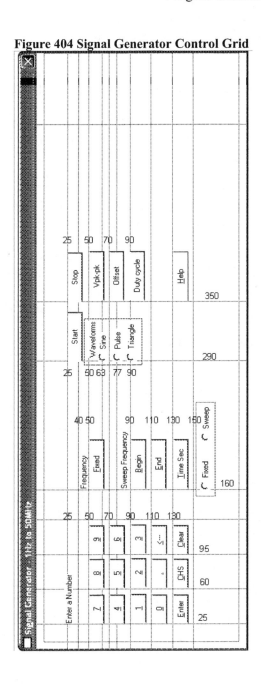

Programming with MFC

## 4.5 Keypad and Code for Programming a Number

The purpose here is to add a 0 to 9 key keypad to the front panel, and the required code that makes the keypad functional; code that activates it.

Each key of the 15 keys in the keypad and the associated code is added to the front panel by the following process, which is shown by example in what follows.

Emphasis: The finished design works as follows.
1) *Enter a Number* (Figure 401). For example the number 1 is entered via the 0 to 9 keypad. Press Enter to end the number entry process.

2) Pressing a push button such as *Begin* produces two actions.
    2.1) The number 1 is stored in the *Begin* register and displayed on the front panel next to the *Begin* push button (Figure 401).
    2.2) The number 1 is sent via the USB bus to program the hardware.

3) After all parameters have been entered press *Start* to emit the periodic signal you programmed. Press *Stop* when you are done.

### 4.5.1 Add a Push Button, Position it, Change Properties

This example adds one push button, digit 7, to the front panel, and the code that activates the button.

Display the *Front Panel* (Figure 401).
Click on left pane *ResourceView* tab. Click on +*SignalGen Resources*
Click on +Dialog. Click on IDD_SIGNALGEN_DIALOG to see the "*Signal Generator 1Hz to 50MHz*" front panel in the right hand pane.

Somewhere on the front panel is a box, the control tool box, containing symbols for the available controls [JP315]. To find out what control a symbol represents let the cursor hover over the symbol for a short time. A ToolTip will appear showing the name of the control associated with the symbol.

4 Signal Generator Front Panel Project

*Add a push button control* [JP319]
Drag a push button from the control tool box onto the front panel
Position the button[1] at coordinates x=25, y=50 (Figure 404).
Click on the button to select it. Reduce button width to 30 units.
Right Click on *Properties*.

**Figure 402**

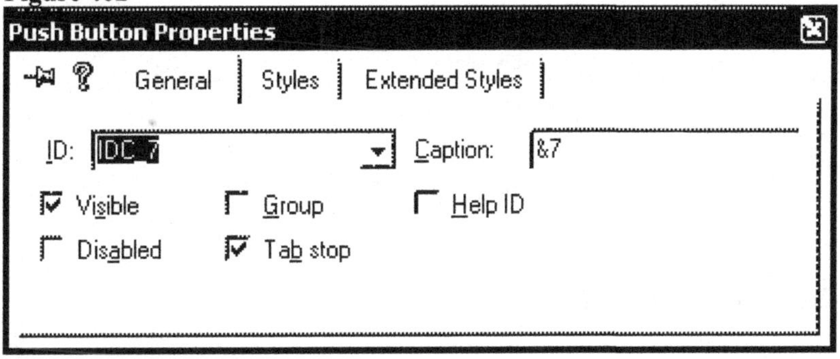

```
Push Button Properties                                    [X]
  General  |  Styles  |  Extended Styles  |

  ID: |IDC_7        ▼|    Caption: |&7

  ☑ Visible      ☐ Group       ☐ Help ID
  ☐ Disabled     ☑ Tab stop
```

In the Push Button Properties dialog box (Figure 402) click on the *General* tab. There are 2 edit boxes *ID* and *Caption*, and 5 check boxes.
    FYI - Get the IDC names from page 19
    In the *ID* edit box erase *IDC_BUTTON*. Type *IDC_7*.
    In the *Caption* edit box type *&7*.
    Only the check boxes *Visible* and *Tab stop* should be checked.
    Click on the X to close the *Push Button Properties* box.

*Add a static text a control that labels the keypad* [JP331]
Drag a static text from the control tool box onto the front panel
Position the static text at coordinates x=25, y=25 (Figure 404).
Right click on the button.
Click on *Properties*.
Click on the *General* tab.
    In the *ID* edit box change nothing.
    In the *Caption* edit box type *Enter a Number*.
    Only the boxes *Visible* and *Group* should be checked.
    Click on the X to close the *Text Properties* box.

> Action –Use copy once to copy button 7. Then use paste and the mouse to position and add a button. Repeat until a total of 15 keypad push buttons are added (Figure 404).

---

[1] 4.4 Position a Control page 14

Programming with MFC

## 4.5.2 Add Push Button Handlers for Message Passing

Click on View, click on Class Wizard, click on Message Maps [JP319].

**Figure 403 Shows that many buttons have been added to the front panel**

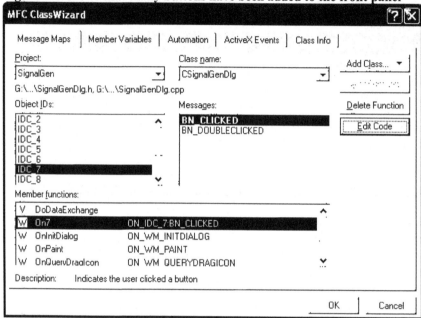

Important: Verify Project is *SignalGen*, Class name is *CSignalGenDlg*
In the *Object IDs* box click on *IDC_7*.
In the *Messages* box click *BN_CLICKED*.
The *Add Function* button is activated.
Click on *Add Function* to get *Add Member function* box. Accept *Member function* name *On7*. Click on OK. This adds code items 1, 2, 3.

1) to *SignalGenDlg.h* a prototype function *afx_msg void On7();*

2) to the message map in *SignalGenDlg.cpp* the function
*ON_BN_CLICKED(IDC_7, On7)*

3) in *SignalGenDlg.cpp* a skeleton message handler
*void CSignalGenDlg::On7()*

# 4 Signal Generator Front Panel Project

> Add the remaining 14 push button handlers

After the 15 key push button message handlers are added the message map in *SignalGenDlg.cpp* includes the following functions.

```
ON_BN_CLICKED(IDC_0, On0)
ON_BN_CLICKED(IDC_1, On1)
ON_BN_CLICKED(IDC_2, On2)
ON_BN_CLICKED(IDC_3, On3)
ON_BN_CLICKED(IDC_4, On4)
ON_BN_CLICKED(IDC_5, On5)
ON_BN_CLICKED(IDC_6, On6)
ON_BN_CLICKED(IDC_7, On7)
ON_BN_CLICKED(IDC_8, On8)
ON_BN_CLICKED(IDC_9, On9)
ON_BN_CLICKED(IDC_ENTER, OnEnter)
ON_BN_CLICKED(IDC_BACKSPACE, OnBackspace)
ON_BN_CLICKED(IDC_CHGSIGN, OnChgsign)
ON_BN_CLICKED(IDC_CLEAR, OnClear)
ON_BN_CLICKED(IDC_DPOINT, OnDpoint)
```

Also see 15 prototypes in file *SignalGenDlg.h* and 15 message handlers in file *SignalGenDlg.cpp*.

Programming with MFC

## 4.5.3 Add Code to Keypad Skeleton Push Button Message Handlers

Many numbers are needed to specify a signal to be generated. This is why we set up the typical number entry push button keypad set: *0 to 9*. The number is displayed in a text box above the keypad. (Figure 401).

**Code 401 Add 3 variables and a define to *SignalGenDlg.h* by hand**

---

```
#define MAXDIGITS    8      // no semicolon in defines
// add 3 variables after public
   BOOL m_bNew;        int m_iNumDigits;        CString m_strNumber;
```

---

> Action–add Code 402 ten times for 0 to 9 to *SignalGenDlg.cpp*

**Code 402 On7( ) - for number buttons 0 to 9 change the 7's – add by hand**

---

```
void CSignalGenDlg::On7()     // the following executes when PB 7 is pressed.
{
  if (m_iNumDigits == MAXDIGITS) {
    AfxMessageBox ("8 digits maximum", MB_OK); // message to output
  }
  else {
    if (m_bNew) {                    // OK to enter a new number
      m_strNumber += (char) 0x37;    // add ASCII char for digit 7 to string
      m_iNumDigits++;                // add 1
      Invalidate (FALSE);            // repaint the window
    }
  }
}
```

---

***MAXDIGITS*** When building a number via a keypad the number of digits in the number needs to be limited for practical reasons. The 50MHz upper limit is why *MAXDIGITS* is defined as 8. *MAXDIGITS* is a symbolic constant defined in *SignalGenDlg.cpp* (Code 401).

To show the advantage of defines, suppose 8 is used 22 times in the code. Then a change from 8 to 10 would require 22 changes of 8 to 10. On the other hand if *MAXDIGITS* is used instead of 8 only ONE change of 8 to 10 implements 22 changes when the *MAXDIGITS* is changed from 8 to 10.

If the current key press of 7 means this 7 is the 8$^{th}$ digit, then when the 7 is stored (by the else statement) *m_iNumDigits* is increased to 8. Any additional digit 0 to 9 will not be stored, because now *m_iNumDigits* = 8 = *MAXDIGITS*.

**BOOL m_bNew**    Only new numbers can be defined.

**int m_iNumDigits**  Stores the number of digits entered into the number.

**CString m_strNumber**  Initially the number is stored as a *string* of characters in *m_strNumber*. The string is converted to a real number by *atof(string)* prior to storage in a number register.

**If–else statement is written as follows:**
if (condition) {
    If the condition is true execute the statements in this body.
}
else {
    If the condition is false execute the statements in this body.
}

**If–else condition** The condition is *m_iNumDigits* == *MAXDIGITS*. In C languages == is the "equals" operator, whereas = is the assignment operator. The condition is true when variable *m_iNumDigits* has value 8, which equals MAXDIGITS.

**Condition-is-true** Then the *if* body emits a message that warns the user.
  AfxMessageBox ("8 digits maximum", MB_OK); // message to output

**Condition-is-false** Then the *else* body processes the digits.
  if (m_bNew) {           // OK to enter a new number
    m_strNumber += (char) 0x37;   // add ASCII char for digit 7 to string
    m_iNumDigits++;       // add 1 to count digits
    Invalidate (FALSE);    // repaint the window
  }

**Message handler *On(7)*** stores the 7 digit as a character in a string of characters *m_strNumber* (an MFC *CString* data type). Digit 7 is stored as a character, because 0x37 is the ASCII[6] code binary word a keyboard emits when key 7 is pressed.

---

[6] ASCII - American Standard Code for Information Interchange

Programming with MFC

**Code 403 Variables, public – add by hand to *SignalGenDlg.h*.**

BOOL m_bDecPt;    int m_iLength;

**Code 404 Decimal Point – add by hand to *SignalGenDlg.cpp*.**

```
void CSignalGenDlg::OnDpoint()
{
  if (m_bDecPt == TRUE) {return ;}   // exit if decimal point is in the number
  m_iLength = m_strNumber.GetLength ();      // get string length

  if (m_iLength == MAXDIGITS) {
    // if max digits do not add any more chars
    AfxMessageBox ("8 digits maximum", MB_OK); // message to output
  }
  else {
    if (m_bNew) {                    // OK to add decimal point
      m_strNumber += (char) 0x2E;    // ASCII code for decimal point [JP444]
      m_bDecPt = TRUE;               // decimal point now in number
      Invalidate (FALSE);            // repaint the window
    }
  }
}
```

Click the keypad *decimal point* button to execute OnDpoint( ). This function is similar to On7( ) where 0x2E (ASCII code for decimal point) replaces 0x37 (ASCII code for 7) and two statements are added.
1) if (m_bDecPt == TRUE) {return;}   // exit if a decimal point is already in the number. A true condition executes *return*, which forces an exit from OnDpoint( ), because only one decimal point is allowed in a number.
2) m_iLength = m_strNumber.GetLength ();      // get string length
Use *CString::GetLength*  // an MFC member of the CString class.

CString object *m_strNumber* uses the dot operator to call any CString member function such as *GetLength*. To discover CString member functions place the Visual C++ cursor over the word CString and press F1.

**Code 405.1 char– add by hand to *SignalGenDlg.h***

CHAR m_char;

22

## 4 Signal Generator Front Panel Project

**Code 405.2 Backspace– add by hand to *SignalGenDlg.cpp***

```
// If backspace removes a digit or decimal point, then m_iNumDigits – 1.
// If backspace removes the decimal point then m_bDecPt = FALSE

void CSignalGenDlg::OnBackspace ()
{
  if (m_bNew) {
    int m_iLength = m_strNumber.GetLength ();   // use GetLength function
    m_char = m_strNumber [m_iLength - 1];        // fetch next char

    if (m_iLength != 0) {
      if (m_char != _T('.')) {
        m_iNumDigits --;
      }
      else {
        m_bDecPt = FALSE;
      }

      m_strNumber = m_strNumber.Left (m_iLength - 1);
      // extracts leftmost m_iLength - 1 chars to store
      Invalidate (FALSE);   // repaint the window
    }
  }
}
```

If *m_bNew* is true we can add digits to, or delete digits from, the number we are building. *GetLength( )* is an MFC CString member function. Use the dot operator to call this member function to get a count of the bytes in this **CString** object. The count does not include a null terminator.

Bytes in a string are numbered from 0, so the last char is at position m_iLength – 1 (e.g. 7 bytes in the string of length 7 are numbered 0 to 6).

Declare *char m_char;*

If the string length is > 0, and if the last char is NOT a dp, then it is a digit that will be removed. So decrease m_iNumDigits by 1. Else the last char is a dp that will be removed. So set m_bDecPt to FALSE. The last char is removed indirectly by rewriting the string with the first m_iLength – 2 chars. Here is the MFC function that does that.
   m_strNumber = m_strNumber.Left (m_iLength – 1);

Programming with MFC

> Action – add 3 variables to *SignalGenDlg.h*
> BOOL m_bEnable;   BOOL m_bPosNumber;   double m_dNumber;

**Code 406 Enter– add by hand to *SignalGenDlg.cpp***

```
void CSignalGenDlg::OnEnter()
{
  m_bEnable = TRUE;           // can store number in any register now
  m_bNew = FALSE;             // cannot build a new number now
  m_iNumDigits = 0;           // prepare for new number
  m_bPosNumber = TRUE;        // ready for new number
  m_bDecPt = FALSE;           // ready for new number
  m_dNumber = atof(m_strNumber);
  // convert number string to floating point double number
  Invalidate (FALSE);
}
```

**Code 407 Change Sign to *SignalGenDlg.cpp*– add by hand**

```
void CSignalGenDlg::OnChgsgn()
{
    if (m_bNew) {
        if (m_bPosNumber == TRUE) {          // if positive do this [JP443]
            m_strNumber = _T ("–") + m_strNumber; // add minus sign to string
            m_bPosNumber = FALSE;                 // number is now negative
        }
        else {                                    // number is negative
            m_iLength = m_strNumber.GetLength (); // use GetLength()
            if (m_iLength != 0) {
            m_strNumber = m_strNumber.Right (m_iLength – 1);
            // delete minus sign by fetching rightmost m_iLength 1 chars
            }
            m_bPosNumber = TRUE;                  // number is now positive
        }
        Invalidate (FALSE);                       // repaint the window
    }
}
```

# 4 Signal Generator Front Panel Project

**Code 408 Add *OnClear* to *SignalGenDlg.cpp* – add by hand**

```
void CSignalGenDlg::OnClear()
{
  m_bNew = TRUE;              //enable storing digits into Number register
  m_iNumDigits = 0;           // ready for new number
  m_bPosNumber = TRUE;        // start with positive number
  m_bDecPt = FALSE;           // start with no decimal point
  m_bEnable = FALSE;          // disable storing a num in any register
  m_strNumber.Empty ();       // empty the number string
  Invalidate (FALSE);         // repaint the window
}
```

## 4.5.4 Initialize Push Button Member Variables

**Code 409 Add by hand to constructor *CSignalGenDlg::CSignalGenDlg*, which follows the *m_hIcon* line in *SignalGenDlg.cpp*.**

```
// init KEYPAD variables
m_bDecPt = FALSE;            // start with no decimal point
m_bEnable = FALSE;           // disable storing digits into any register
m_bNew = TRUE;               // enable storing digits into Number register
m_bPosNumber = TRUE;         // start with positive number
m_iLength = 0;               // start with no char in string
m_iNumDigits = 0;            // start with empty string
m_strNumber = _T("654321");
```

| Variable | Reason why it is included |
|---|---|
| MAXDIGITS 8 | A define. It is always prudent to limit number size. |
| m_iNumDigits | MAXDIGITS requires counting digits. |
| m_bPosNumber | Since sign can be changed by toggling the button CHS the current sign is saved. |
| m_bDecPt | Decimal point status also has to be saved. |
| m_strNumber | A CString variable storing the number. Each time we click on a 0 to 9 PB the corresponding digit ASCII code is added to a string. See (char) 0x37 code 401. |
| m_iNumDigits | Add 1 when digit count is incremented. |
| int m_iLength | Adding 0 to 9, period, and sign char change length. |
| m_bNew | Can enter a new number |
| m_char | Stores a keypad ASCII character |
| m_bDecPt | Decimal point is in the number |
| m_bEnable | Can store the number in any register now |

## Programming with MFC

### 4.5.5 Add *OnPaint* Code

Find *OnPaint*: A straightforward way to find *OnPaint* is to click on *ClassView* in the Visual C++ left pane. Then click on *+CSignalGenDlg* to see all functions. Find *OnPaint* in the list and click on it.

*WaveformScreen* function (page 41) paints the waveform screen on the front panel. Pressing a waveform button (sine, pulse, triangle) erases any waveform on the screen, and paints the selected waveform (sine, pulse, triangle) on the waveform screen.

Numbers are placed in text boxes. A brush specifies the text box color. The font is the device context default font.

Text box coordinates are specified. They are used to define a device context rectangle. *Rectangle* and *TextOut* are MFC functions.

**Code 410 Add by hand to *OnPaint* in *SignalGenDlg.cpp*. Delete** *if (IsIconic)*.

```
void CSignalGenDlg::OnPaint()
{
    CPaintDC dc(this);                              // device context for painting
    // select rectangles' body brush color
    CBrush brush (RGB (255, 255, 213));             // [JP64]
    CBrush* pOldBrush = dc.SelectObject (&brush);   // [JP43]
    // Initialize the device context.
    dc.SetTextAlign (TA_RIGHT | TA_BOTTOM);         // [JP67]
    dc.SetBkMode (TRANSPARENT);                     // [JP43]
    // keypad
    int x1 = 37, dx1 = 80;
    int y1 = 60, dy1 = 17, dy11 = 16;
    dc.Rectangle (x1, y1, x1+dx1, y1+dy1);          // the body of the Number display
    dc.TextOut (x1+dx1, y1+dy11, m_strNumber);      // print the Number
}
```

## 4.6 Code for Programming a Frequency

Add controls to the front panel that program the signal generator frequency: push buttons, *Fixed, Begin, End,* and *Time Sec*, radio buttons *Fixed,* and *Sweep*, and static texts *Frequency* and *Sweep Frequency* (Figure 404, page 15).

To add buttons copy the process in Sections 4.5.1 and 4.5.2 pages 16 and 18. Use the IDC names in 3) below.

Button program additions
1) 6 buttons to the front panel

2) 6 prototypes to *SignalGenDlg.h*
   afx_msg void OnBegin();
   afx_msg void OnEnd();
   afx_msg void OnFixed();
   afx_msg void OnRfixed();
   afx_msg void OnRsweep();
   afx_msg void OnTimesec();

3) 6 functions to the message map in *SignalGenDlg.cpp*.
   ON_BN_CLICKED(IDC_FIXED, OnFixed)        push buttons
   ON_BN_CLICKED(IDC_BEGIN, OnBegin)
   ON_BN_CLICKED(IDC_END, OnEnd)
   ON_BN_CLICKED(IDC_TIMESEC, OnTimesec)
   ON_BN_CLICKED(IDC_RFIXED, OnRfixed)      radio button
   ON_BN_CLICKED(IDC_RSWEEP, OnRsweep)      radio button

4) 6 functions to *SignalGenDlg.cpp*
   *OnFixed, OnBegin, OnEnd, OnTimeSec, OnRsweep, OnRFixed*

How it works:
1) Use the keypad to create the fixed frequency number. Click on the *Fixed* radio button. After *Enter* is pressed, press the *Fixed* push button to store the number in the *Fixed* frequency register.

If a signal frequency is to be swept over a range of frequencies click on the *Sweep* radio button. Then the beginning and end frequency numbers are created via the keypad and stored in the *Begin* and *End* frequency registers.

Create, via the keypad, the beginning-to-end sweep time number. Store it in the *Time sec* register.

# Programming with MFC

> Action – add 2 variables to *SignalGenDlg.h*
> double m_dFixed;   CString m_strFixed;

**Code 411 Fixed Frequency– add by hand to *SignalGenDlg.cpp*.**

```
void CSignalGenDlg::OnFixed()
{
  if (m_bEnable) {
    m_strFixed = m_strNumber;           // transfer number to Fixed
    m_strNumber.Empty ();               // erase the number in the string
    m_dFixed = atof(m_strFixed);        // convert number to a floating point double

    if (m_dFixed < 0) {                 // if the number is negative make it positive
      m_iLength = m_strFixed.GetLength ();
      if (m_iLength != 0) {
        m_strFixed = m_strFixed.Right (m_iLength – 1);   // extracts chars
      }
    }

    m_dFixed = atof(m_strFixed);        // convert string to f point double number

    if (m_dFixed < 1) {                 // if the number is <1 make it = 1.
      m_strFixed = _T("1");
      m_dFixed = atof(m_strFixed);
    }
  }

// add code here that sends m_iNumber to siggen device via USB channel.
    m_bEnable = FALSE;                  // disable programming
    m_bNew = TRUE;                      // enable entering a new number
    Invalidate (FALSE);                 // repaint the window
}
```

> Action – add 2 variables to *SignalGenDlg.h*
> double m_dBegin;   CString m_strBegin;

**Code 412 Begin Frequency– add by hand to *SignalGenDlg.cpp***

```
void CSignalGenDlg::OnBegin()
// same as OnFixed. Just replace m_strFixed with m_strBegin
// and m_dFixed with m_dBegin.
```

## 4 Signal Generator Front Panel Project

> Action – add 2 variables to *SignalGenDlg.h*
> double m_dEnd;    CString m_strEnd;

### Code 413 End Frequency– add by hand to *SignalGenDlg.cpp*

void CSignalGenDlg::OnEnd()
// same as OnFixed. Just replace m_strFixed with m_strEnd
// and m_dFixed with m_dEnd.

> Action – add 2 variables to *SignalGenDlg.h*
> double m_dTsec;    CString m_strTsec;

### Code 414 Time Sec– add by hand to *SignalGenDlg.cpp*

// add   #include "math.h" to *SignalGenDlg.cpp*

```
void CSignalGenDlg::OnTimesec()
{
   if (m_bEnable) {
       m_strTsec = m_strNumber;          // transfer number to time sec
       m_strNumber.Empty ();             // erase the number
       m_dTsec = atof(m_strTsec);        //convert number to a floating point double

       if (m_dTsec > 50)
       { m_strTsec = _T("50");}          // limit time to 50 seconds
       if (m_dTsec < –50)
       { m_strTsec = _T("50");}          // make time number positive

       m_dTsec = atof(m_strTsec);        //convert number to a floating point double
       if (m_dTsec < 0.0) {              // remove the minus sign
         m_dTsec = fabs (m_dTsec);       //get absolute value of floating point
         m_iLength = m_strTsec.GetLength ();
         if (m_iLength != 0)
         {m_strTsec = m_strTsec.Right (m_iLength – 1) ;} // extracts chars
       }
   }
```

// **add code here that sends m_dTsec to siggen device via USB channel.**

```
   m_bEnable = FALSE;
   m_bNew = TRUE;
   Invalidate (FALSE);
}
```

# Programming with MFC

### Code 415 Rsweep– add by hand to *SignalGenDlg.cpp*

```
void CSignalGenDlg::OnRsweep()
{
    MessageBox("add code here that sends SWEEP FREQUENCY to siggen device via USB channel", "To USB", MB_OK);
}
```

### Code 416 Rfixed– add by hand to *SignalGenDlg.cpp*

```
void CSignalGenDlg::OnRfixed()
{
    MessageBox("add code here that sends FIXED FREQUENCY to siggen device via USB channel", "To USB", MB_OK);
}
```

### Code 417 Initialized Variables– add by hand to constructor *CSignalGenDlg::CSignalGenDlg* in *SignalGenDlg.cpp*

```
// FREQUENCIES  code 417
  m_dFixed = 555000;
  m_dBegin = 1;
  m_dEnd = 100000;
  m_dTsec = 10;
  m_strFixed = _T("555000");
  m_strBegin = _T("1");
  m_strEnd = _T("100000");
  m_strTsec = _T("10");
```

CString member function *Right (m_iLength – 1)* only copies char to the right of the minus sign effectively deleting it. *m_iLength – 1* is the number of characters to extract from the *m_strFixed* CString object

30

**Code 418 Add to OnPaint by hand in *SignalGenDlg.cpp***

```cpp
// Frequency code 418
    int x2 = 325, dx2 = 80, y2 = 85, dy2 = 20, dy22 = 18;
    int y3 = 150, dy3 = 20, dy33 = 18;

    // B1-Draw the body of the Fixed display.
    dc.Rectangle (x2, y2, x2+dx2, y2+dy2);
    // B1-print the fixed frequency
    dc.TextOut (x2+dx2-5, y2+dy22, m_strFixed);
    // --------------------
    // B2-Draw the body of the Begin display.
    dc.Rectangle (x2, y3, x2+dx2, y3+dy3);
    // B2-print the begin frequency
    dc.TextOut (x2+dx2-5, y3+dy33, m_strBegin);
    //--------------------
    // B3-Draw the body of the End display.
    dc.Rectangle (x2, y3+32, x2+dx2, y3+32+dy3);
    // B3-print the end frequency
    dc.TextOut (x2+dx2-5, y3+32+dy33, m_strEnd);
    //--------------------
    // B4-Draw the body of the Tsec display.
    dc.Rectangle (x2, y3+64, x2+dx2, y3+64+dy3);
    // B4-print Tsec
    dc.TextOut (x2+dx2-5, y3+64+dy33, m_strTsec);
```

Programming with MFC

# 4.7 Code for Programming a Waveform

Action - Add, to the front panel, three radio buttons, *Sine, Pulse, Triangle*, three push buttons *Vpk pk, Offset, Duty Cycle* that program the signal generator amplitude and duty cycle (Figure 404, page 15). Then add *Start* and *Stop* buttons.

To add buttons copy the process in Sections 4.5.1 and 4.5.2 pages 16 and 18.

Button programming additions
1) 8 buttons to the front panel

2) 8 prototypes to *SignalGenDlg.h*
```
afx_msg void OnSine();
afx_msg void OnPulse();
afx_msg void OnTriangle();
afx_msg void OnVpkpk();
afx_msg void OnOffset();
afx_msg void OnDutyCycle();
afx_msg void OnStart();
afx_msg void OnStop();
```

3) 8 functions to the message map in *SignalGenDlg.cpp*.
```
ON_BN_CLICKED(IDC_SINE, OnSine)
ON_BN_CLICKED(IDC_PULSE, OnPulse)
ON_BN_CLICKED(IDC_TRIANGLE, OnTriangle)
ON_BN_CLICKED(IDC_VPKPK, OnVpkpk)
ON_BN_CLICKED(IDC_OFFSET, OnOffset)
ON_BN_CLICKED(IDC_DUTYCYCLE, OnDutyCycle)
ON_BN_CLICKED(IDC_START, OnStart)
ON_BN_CLICKED(IDC_STOP, OnStop)
```

4) 8 functions to *SignalGenDlg.cpp*
*OnSine, OnPulse, OnTriangle, OnVpkpk, OnOffset, OnDutyCycle, OnStart, OnStop*

---

Action - Add a group box control enclosing radio buttons, *Sine, Pulse, Triangle* [JP323]. Change Group box properties. Change caption to Waveforms. Check the Group box.

Change Sine properties [JP322 items 1,2,3]. Check the Group box.

# 4 Signal Generator Front Panel Project

The waveform functions *Sine, Pulse, Triangle* are selected in *OnPaint* by a true *if* condition. The *if* condition is set in functions *OnSine, OnPulse, OnTriangle* (Codes 419, 420, and 421).

> Action – add 3 variables to *SignalGenDlg.h*
> BOOL m_bSine;   BOOL m_bPulse;   BOOL m_bTriangle;

### Code 419 OnSine– add by hand to *SignalGenDlg.cpp*

```
void CSignalGenDlg::OnSine( )
  {
  m_bSine = 1;        // select sine
  m_bPulse = 0;
  m_bTriangle = 0;
  Invalidate (FALSE);
  }
```

### Code 420 OnPulse– add by hand to *SignalGenDlg.cpp*

```
void CSignalGenDlg::OnPulse()
{
  m_bSine = 0;
  m_bPulse = 1;       // select pulse
  m_bTriangle = 0;
  Invalidate (FALSE);
}
```

### Code 421 OnTriangle– add by hand to *SignalGenDlg.cpp*

```
void CSignalGenDlg::OnTriangle()
{
  m_bSine = 0;
  m_bPulse = 0;
  m_bTriangle = 1;    // select triangle
  Invalidate (FALSE);
}
```

Programming with MFC

> Action – add 2 variables to *SignalGenDlg.h*
> double m_dVpp;      CString m_strVpp;

**Code 422 Vpkpk – add by hand to *SignalGenDlg.cpp***

```
void CSignalGenDlg::OnVpkpk()
{
    if (m_bEnable) {
      m_strVpp = m_strNumber;
      m_strNumber.Empty ();
      m_dVpp = atof(m_strVpp);
      if (m_dVpp > 2.0)          // peak to peak voltage limit to ± 2 volts max
         { m_strVpp = _T("2");}
      if (m_dVpp < –2.0)
         { m_strVpp = _T("2");}
      m_dVpp = atof(m_strVpp);

      if (m_dVpp < 0.0)   // remove the minus sign
      {
         m_dVpp = fabs(m_dVpp);
         m_iLength = m_strVpp.GetLength ();
         if (m_iLength != 0)
         {m_strVpp = m_strVpp.Right (m_iLength – 1) ;}
      }
      // add code that sends m_dVpp to siggen device via USB channel.
      m_bEnable = FALSE;
      m_bNew = TRUE;
      Invalidate (FALSE);
   }
}
```

**Code 423 Add OnStart() to *SignalGenDlg.cpp* by hand**

```
void CSignalGenDlg::OnStart()
{    MessageBox("add code here that sends START to siggen
     device via USB channel", "To USB", MB_OK);   }
```

**Code 424 – Add OnStop() to *SignalGenDlg.cpp* by hand**

```
void CSignalGenDlg::OnStop()
{    MessageBox("add code here that sends STOP to siggen
     device via USB channel", "To USB", MB_OK);   }
```

# 4 Signal Generator Front Panel Project

> Action – add 2 variables to *SignalGenDlg.h*
> *double m_dOffset;   CString m_strOffset;*

**Code 425 Add Offset() to *SignalGenDlg.cpp* by hand**

```
void CSignalGenDlg::OnOffset()
{
    if (m_bEnable) {
      m_strOffset = m_strNumber;
      m_strNumber.Empty ();
      m_dOffset = atof(m_strOffset);

      if (m_dOffset > 1.0)          // offset limited to –1 volt to +1 volt range
      { m_strOffset = _T("1");}

      if (m_dOffset < –1.0)
      { m_strOffset = _T("–1");}

      m_dOffset = atof(m_strOffset);
      // add code that sends m_dOffset to siggen device via USB channel.
      m_bEnable = FALSE;
      m_bNew = TRUE;
      Invalidate (FALSE);
    }
}
```

> Action – add 2 variables to *SignalGenDlg.h*
> *double m_dDutyCycle;   CString m_strDutyCycle;*

**Code 426 Add Duty Cycle to *SignalGenDlg.cpp* by hand**

```
void CSignalGenDlg::OnDutycycle()
{
    if (m_bEnable) {
      m_strDutyCycle = m_strNumber;
      m_strNumber.Empty ();
      m_dDutyCycle = atof(m_strDutyCycle);

      if (m_dDutyCycle > 90)     // duty cycle limited to 10% to 90% range
      { m_strDutyCycle = _T("90");}

      if (m_dDutyCycle < 10)
      { m_strDutyCycle = _T("10");}
```

Programming with MFC

```
        m_dDutyCycle = atof(m_strDutyCycle);
        // add code here that sends m_dDutyCycle to siggen device.
        m_bEnable = FALSE;
        m_bNew = TRUE;
        Invalidate (FALSE);
    }
}
```

**Code 427 Initialized Variables– add by hand to constructor *CSignalGenDlg::CSignalGenDlg* in *SignalGenDlg.cpp***

```
// WAVEFORMS code 427
  m_dVpp = 2;
  m_dOffset = 0;
  m_dDutyCycle = 30;
  m_strVpp = _T("2");
  m_strOffset = _T("0");
  m_strDutyCycle = _T("30");
  m_bSine = 0;
  m_bPulse = 0;
  m_bTriangle = 0;
```

**Code 428 Add waveforms OnPaint in *SignalGenDlg.cpp* by hand**

```
// Waveforms code 428
  int x4 = 610, dx4 = 40, y4 = 85, dy4 = 20, dy44 = 18;
  // C1-Draw the body of the Vpp display.
  dc.Rectangle (x4, y4, x4+dx4, y4+dy4);
  // C1-print Vpp
  dc.TextOut (x4+dx4–5, y4+dy44, m_strVpp);
    // C2-Draw the body of the Offset display.
    dc.Rectangle (x4, y4+32, x4+dx4, y4+32+dy4);
    // C2-print the offset
    dc.TextOut (x4+dx4–5, y4+32+dy44, m_strOffset);
  // C3-Draw the body of the Duty Cycle display.
  dc.Rectangle (x4, y4+64, x4+dx4, y4+64+dy4);
  // C3-print the duty cycle
  dc.TextOut (x4+dx4–5, y4+64+dy44, m_strDutyCycle);
```

## 4.8 Functions that support the Waveform Display

The front panel waveform display does not program the hardware. The display is a convenience for the user.
All waveforms have 2 volt peak to peak maximum amplitude.
Voltage offset is restricted to ±1 Volt.
Duty cycle is restricted to 10% to 90% range.

**Code 429 Add Waveform defines to *SignalGenDlg.cpp* by hand**

```
#define u0  750      // screen coordinates
#define v0 –80
#define u1 950
#define v1 –240
#define HOUT 10
#define VOUT 8
```

Class Wizard **cannot** assist with waveform support functions.

**Code 430 Add Function Prototypes to *SignalGenDlg.h* by hand**

```
void Sine (BOOL m_bSine, double m_dOffset, double m_dVpp);
void Pulse (BOOL m_bPulse, double m_dOffset, double m_dVpp, double m_dDutyCycle);
void Triangle (BOOL m_bTriangle, double m_dOffset, double m_dVpp);
void WaveformScreen ();
```

Plots are more easily programmed if plots are deviations from zero. Therefore max volts dv=m_Vpp/2   dv=1 max.
And, max volts offset df=-m_dOffset/4 * (v1–v0),
so that max df = –1/4*(–195+35) =40 or 1 volt equivalent

The sine function defines the sine waveform.
Sine[j].x = u0+ (j * (u1–u0) / SEGMENTS) = 600+ (j*200)/10000
so that x ranges from 600 to 800 in 10,000 steps.

Sine[j].y = [df+v0+ (v1–v0)/2] + [dv * (v1–v0)/4 *–sin (4 * PI * j/SEGMENTS)] = [40–35–160/2] + [1*(–160)/4*–sin (4 PI j/10000)]
        = –75+40 sin (4 PI j/10000)
where
for two waveforms (4 PI j/10000) ranges from 0 to 4 cycles, and the –75 puts the waveform zero in the vertical center of the output box.

Programming with MFC

**Code 431 Add Sine to *SignalGenDlg.cpp* by hand**

```
#define SEGMENTS 10000      // waveform constants
#define PI 3.1415926
#define PULSE 9
#define TRIANGLE 5

void CSignalGenDlg::Sine (BOOL m_bSine, double m_dOffset, double m_dVpp)
  // [JP 55]  code 431
{
   if (m_bSine == 1)
    {
    CClientDC dc (this);
    dc.SetMapMode (MM_LOENGLISH);
    CPen pen1 (PS_SOLID, 2, RGB (0, 0, 0,));            // [JP 60, 61]
    CPen* pOldPen1 = dc.SelectObject (&pen1);

    double dv = m_dVpp/2;
    double df = -m_dOffset/4 * (v1–v0);
    CPoint Sine[SEGMENTS];

    for (int j=0; j<SEGMENTS; j++)
     {
      Sine[j].x = u0+(j * (u1-u0) / SEGMENTS );
      Sine[j].y = df+v0+ (v1–v0)/2+ dv * (v1–v0)/4 * –sin (4 * PI * j/SEGMENTS);
     }
    dc.Polyline (Sine, SEGMENTS);
    }
   return;
}
```

## 4 Signal Generator Front Panel Project

An array of points defines the pulse waveform. The function *dc.Polyline (Pulse, PULSE)* draws from point to point to produce the waveform.

**Code 432 Add Pulse to *SignalGenDlg.cpp* by hand**

```
void CSignalGenDlg::Pulse (BOOL m_bPulse, double m_dOffset, double
m_dVpp, double m_dDutyCycle)
{
// pulse  code 433
  if (m_bPulse == 1)   {
    CClientDC dc (this);
    dc.SetMapMode (MM_LOENGLISH);

    CPen pen1 (PS_SOLID, 2, RGB (0, 0, 0,));  //P 60, 61
    CPen* pOldPen1 = dc.SelectObject (&pen1);
    double dv = m_dVpp/2;
    double df = -m_dOffset/4 * (v1-v0);
    double ddc = m_dDutyCycle/100;
    double dx = (u1-u0)/2;
    double dy = ((v1-v0)/4)*dv;

    CPoint Pulse [PULSE];
    Pulse[0].x = u0;
    Pulse[1].x = u0;
    Pulse[2].x = u0+1*dx*ddc;
    Pulse[3].x = u0+1*dx*ddc;
    Pulse[4].x = u0+1*dx;
    Pulse[5].x = u0+1*dx;
    Pulse[6].x = u0+1*dx+1*dx*ddc;
    Pulse[7].x = u0+1*dx+1*dx*ddc;
    Pulse[8].x = u0+2*dx;
    Pulse [0].y = df+v0+ (v1-v0)/2+dy;
    Pulse [1].y = df+v0+ (v1-v0)/2-dy;
    Pulse [2].y = df+v0+ (v1-v0)/2-dy;
    Pulse [3].y = df+v0+ (v1-v0)/2+dy;
    Pulse [4].y = df+v0+ (v1-v0)/2+dy;
    Pulse [5].y = df+v0+ (v1-v0)/2-dy;
    Pulse [6].y = df+v0+ (v1-v0)/2-dy;
    Pulse [7].y = df+v0+ (v1-v0)/2+dy;
    Pulse [8].y = df+v0+ (v1-v0)/2+dy;
    dc.Polyline (Pulse, PULSE);
  }
  return;
}
```

Programming with MFC

An array of points defines the triangle waveform. The function *dc.Polyline (Triangle, TRIANGLE)* draws from point to point to produce the waveform.

**Code 433 Add Triangle to *SignalGenDlg.cpp* by hand**

```
void CSignalGenDlg::Triangle (BOOL m_bTriangle, double m_dOffset, double m_dVpp)
{   // triangle code 434
  if (m_bTriangle == 1)
  {
    CClientDC dc (this);
    dc.SetMapMode (MM_LOENGLISH);

    CPen pen1 (PS_SOLID, 2, RGB (0, 0, 0,));   //P 60, 61
    CPen* pOldPen1 = dc.SelectObject (&pen1);
    double dv = m_dVpp/2;
    double df = -m_dOffset/4 * (v1-v0);
    double dx = (u1-u0)/4;
    double dy = ((v1-v0)/4)*dv;

    CPoint Triangle[TRIANGLE];
    Triangle[0].x = u0;
    Triangle[1].x = u0+dx;
    Triangle[2].x = u0+2*dx;
    Triangle[3].x = u0+3*dx;
    Triangle[4].x = u0+4*dx;

    Triangle [0].y = df+v0+ (v1-v0)/2+dy;      //v0+3*dy+df;
    Triangle [1].y = df+v0+ (v1-v0)/2-dy;      //v0+1*dy+df;
    Triangle [2].y = df+v0+ (v1-v0)/2+dy;      //v0+3*dy+df;
    Triangle [3].y = df+v0+ (v1-v0)/2-dy;      //v0+1*dy+df;
    Triangle [4].y = df+v0+ (v1-v0)/2+dy;      //v0+3*dy+df;
    dc.Polyline (Triangle, TRIANGLE);
  }
  return;
}
```

**Code 434 Add WaveformScreen to *SignalGenDlg.cpp* by hand**

```
void CSignalGenDlg::WaveformScreen()  // code 435
{
  CClientDC dc (this);
  dc.SetMapMode (MM_LOENGLISH);
  dc.SetTextAlign (TA_RIGHT | TA_BOTTOM);
```

# 4 Signal Generator Front Panel Project

```
    dc.SetBkMode (TRANSPARENT);
// select body brush color
    CBrush brush (RGB (255, 255, 213));
    CBrush* pOldBrush = dc.SelectObject (&brush);
// draw output   // create gray solid pen
    CPen pen0 (PS_SOLID, 1, RGB (130, 130, 130,));  //light gray P 60, 61
    CPen* pOldPen0 = dc.SelectObject (&pen0);    //Prosise 60
// K-Draw the body of the Output display and  print Output
    dc.Rectangle (u0, v0, u1, v1);
// dc.TextOut (u0+100, v0+2, "Output Voltage");
// Draw H and V lines
    int dx= (u1- u0)/HOUT;
    int dy= (v1- v0)/VOUT;
    int i;
// H-Draw the Output horizontal lines.
    for (i=1; i<VOUT; i++) {
       dc.MoveTo(u0, v0+(dy*i));
       dc.LineTo(u1, v0+(dy*i));
    }
// V-Draw the Output vertical lines.
    for (i=1; i<HOUT; i++) {
       dc.MoveTo(u0+(dx*i), v0);
       dc.LineTo(u0+(dx*i), v1);
    }
    CPen pen1 (PS_SOLID, 1, RGB (0, 0, 0,));   //P 60, 61  // add black solid pen
    CPen* pOldPen1 = dc.SelectObject (&pen1);
// H-Draw Zero line.
    dc.MoveTo(u0, v0+(dy*4));
    dc.LineTo(u1, v0+(dy*4));
    // draw output voltage scale
    dc.TextOut (u0-5, v0-10, "2");
    dc.TextOut (u0-5, v0-50, "1");
    dc.TextOut (u0-5, v0-90, "0");
    dc.TextOut (u0-6, v0-128, "-1");
    dc.TextOut (u0-6, v0-165, "-2");
    return;
} //end of WaveformScreen
```

**Code 435 Add Functions to OnPaint in *SignalGenDlg.cpp* by hand**

```
WaveformScreen();
Sine (m_bSine, m_dOffset, m_dVpp);
Pulse (m_bPulse, m_dOffset, m_dVpp, m_dDutyCycle);
Triangle (m_bTriangle, m_dOffset, m_dVpp);
```

Programming with MFC

## 4.9 A Simple Help Program

Add a Help push button per pages 16 and 18. Use IDC_HELP1.
Click on *View*, click on *Class Wizard*, click on *Message Maps*.
Check project is *SignalGen*, class name is *CSignalGenDlg*
In the *Object Ids* box click on *IDC_HELP1*
In the *Messages* box click *BN_CLICKED*.
Click on *Add Function* to add *OnHelp1*.
Click on *Edit Code* to see the function is a skeleton message handler.
The *Add Function* button is activated.
Click on *Add Function* to get *Add Member function* box. Accept *Member function* name *OnHelp1*. Click on OK. This adds the code items 1, 2, 3.

**Code 436 Add OnRButtonDown to *SignalGenDlg.cpp* by hand**

```
{
    CString strRightClick ;
    strRightClick = (CString)
    "Click on Clear to erase Number register and allow entry of a new number."
    + "\n"
    + "Click on 0 to 9 to enter digits."
    + "\n"
    + "Click on . (dot) to enter a decimal point."
    + "\n"
    + "Click on <- to delete digits."
    + "\n"
    + "Click on CHS to change sign of number."
    + "\n"
    + "Click on Enter to enable storing a number in a parameter register."
    + "\n"
    + "Click any parameter button to store a parameter in the appropriate register."
    + "\n"
    + "Such as Fixed, Begin, or End to store a frequency in Fixed, Start, or End registers."
    + "\n"
    + "The max number of digits is 8. However max frequency is 50MHz"
    + "\n";
    MessageBox(strRightClick,"Click on buttons", MB_OK);
    CDialog::OnRButtonDown(nFlags, point);
}
```

## 4.10 Summary: Variables, Initialize Variables

Recapitulation of added variables to *SignalGenDlg.h*
class CSignalGenDlg : public CDialog

public:
    int m_cxChar;
    int m_cyChar;
    CFont m_fontMain;
    CFont m_fontMain1;

    BOOL m_bNew;
    BOOL m_bPosNumber;
    BOOL m_bEnable;
    BOOL m_bDecPt;

    int m_iLength;
    int m_iNumDigits;
    char m_char;
    double m_dNumber;

    double m_dFixed;
    double m_dBegin;
    double m_dEnd;
    double m_dTsec;

    double m_dNum;
    long m_lNum;
    long m_iNumber[40];

    double m_dVpp;
    double m_dOffset;
    double m_dDutyCycle;
    BOOL m_bSine;
    BOOL m_bPulse;
    BOOL m_bTriangle;

CString m_strNumber;    CString m_strFixed;    CString m_strBegin;
CString m_strEnd;    CString m_strTsec;    CString m_strDbmax;
CString m_strDbmin;    CString m_strDegmax;    CString m_strDegmin;
CString m_strVpp;    CString m_strOffset;    CString m_strDutyCycle;

Programming with MFC

Initialized variables in *SignalGenDlg.cpp*
```
// CSignalGenDlg dialog
CSignalGenDlg::CSignalGenDlg(CWnd* pParent /*=NULL*/)
    : CDialog(CSignalGenDlg::IDD, pParent)
{
// init variables
    m_bNew = TRUE;            // enable storing digits into Number register
    m_bPosNumber = TRUE;
    m_bDecPt = FALSE;
    m_iNumDigits = 0;
    m_bEnable = FALSE;        // disable storing digits into any register

    m_dFixed = 555000;        // prevent program exit if no parameter.
    m_dBegin = 1;
    m_dEnd = 100000;
    m_dTsec = 10;

    m_dVpp = 2;               // show waveform parameters
    m_dOffset = 0;
    m_dDutyCycle = 30;
    m_dDbmax = 0;
    m_dDbmin = –50;

    m_strNumber = _T("");
    m_strFixed = _T("555000");
    m_strBegin = _T("1");
    m_strEnd = _T("100000");
    m_strTsec = _T("10");

    m_strVpp = _T("2");
    m_strOffset = _T("0");
    m_strDutyCycle = _T("30");
}
```

# 5 Oscilloscope Front Panel Project

The intent is to design a two channel digital storage oscilloscope. The front panel contains the following controls (Figure 501).

1 Waveform screen display
    Voltage 8 vertical divisions
    Time 10 horizontal divisions.

2 Vertical controls – identical for 2 channels
    Select AC, DC, Ground – the channel input coupling.
    Select display screen Volts/Division – 2mv to 5v per division
    2, 5, 10, 20, 50, 100, 200, 500 mv per division
    1, 2, 5 volts per division.
    vertical position of zero volt sweep level

3. Sweep – Seconds/Division - time per division 5ns to 50s per division
    2, 5, 10, 20, 50, 100, 200, 500 ns per division
    1, 2, 5, 10, 20, 50, 100, 200, 500 ms per division
    1, 2, 5, 10, 20, 50 s per division
    Horizontal position of sweep

4. Trigger controls
    Select Trigger Source
        Channel 1, 2 AC or DC, AC line, external
    Select Trigger Type
        edge rise, edge fall, pulse normal, pulse inverted
    Select Norm, Auto trigger or View to see the trigger
    Select Level the amplitude level that the signal must cross to acquire a waveform.
    Position trigger level.

6. Menus - push buttons display specific menus to select from.
    Acquire, Cursor, Display, Filter, Math, Measure, Save/Load, Utility

7. Signal - push buttons select signal mode.
    Single, Run, Stop, Help

Programming with MFC

## 5.1 Create a dialog based project workspace.

Follow the procedure in Chapter 1, Section 1.3 except as follows.
    Type the name *Oscilloscope* in the *Project Name* edit box.
    Note addition of *Oscilloscope* in the *Location* edit box.
    In step 2 of 4 type the title *Digital Storage Oscilloscope 50 MHz*

## 5.2 Build the *Oscilloscope* Project

Follow the procedure in Chapter 1, Section 1.4, page 4.

## 5.3 Change Dialog size and delete the OK and Cancel Buttons

Click on *File*, click on *Open* to get the *Open* dialog box
Change contents of the *Open as* edit box to *Text*
Click on *Oscilloscope.rc*
Click on Open to open the *.rc* file
Go to the file's *Dialog* section, and change
from
IDD_OSCILLOSCOPE_DIALOG DIALOGEX  0, 0, 320, 200
to
IDD_OSCILLOSCOPE_DIALOG DIALOGEX  0, 0, 675, 300

Click on File, click on *Save as* to get *Save as* dialog box, click on *Save*.
Close the *Oscilloscope.rc* file.

Click *ResourceView* at bottom of left pane.
Click on +Oscilloscope Resources.
Click on + Dialog.
Click on IDD_OSCILLOSCOPE_DIALOG.
Observe the new size of the dialog box (the front panel).

Click on the *OK* button. Right click, select cut to remove button
Click on the *Cancel* button. Right click, select cut to remove button
Click on the *text*. Right click, select cut to remove the text.

> *Emphasis: The dialog box is the front panel*

# 5 Oscilloscope Front Panel Project

**Figure 501 Oscilloscope Front Panel Design**

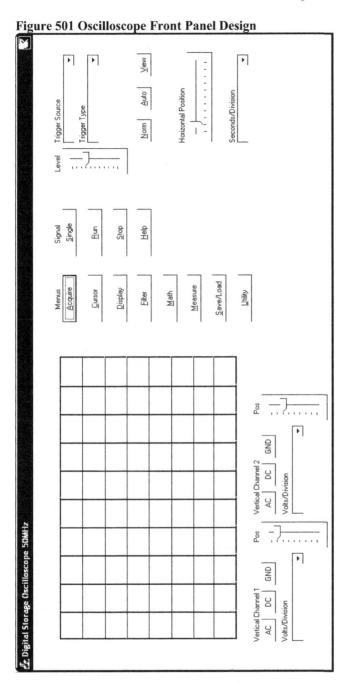

Programming with MFC

**Figure 509 Grid for Oscilloscope Controls**

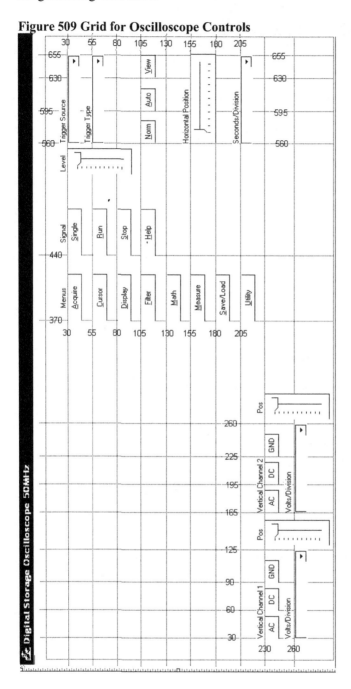

# 5 Oscilloscope Front Panel Project

## 5.4 Code for Adding a Push Button

Show the *Front Panel* (Figure 501).
Click on left pane *ResourceView* tab. Click on +Oscilloscope Resources. Click on +Dialog. Click on IDD_OSCILLOSCOPE_DIALOG to see the "*Digital Storage Oscilloscope 50 MHz*" front panel in the right hand pane.

Somewhere on the front panel is a box, the control tool box, containing symbols for the available controls [JP315]. To find out what control a symbol represents let the cursor hover over the symbol for a short time. A ToolTip will appear showing the name of the control associated with the symbol.

*Add a control - push button example* [JP319]
  Drag a push button from the control tool box onto the front panel
  Position the button[1] as the *Acquire* button (Figures 501, 509).
  Right click on the button.
  Click on *Properties*.

**Figure 502**

In the Push Button Properties dialog box (Figure 502) click on the *General* tab. There are 2 edit boxes *ID* and *Caption*, and 5 check boxes.
  In the *Caption* edit box type &*Acquire*. This is the push button title.
  In the *ID* edit box erase IDC_BUTTON. Type IDC_ACQUIRE .
  Only the check boxes *Visible* and *Tab stop* should be checked.
  Click on the X to close the *Push Button Properties* box.
  Note: if a button is the first button in a group check the group box.

| Action – add 8 menu and 4 signal push buttons (Figure 509). |
|---|

---
[1] 4.4 Position a Control page 14

49

Programming with MFC

> Action – add 8 menu and 4 signal message handlers (Figure 509).

Click on View, click on Class Wizard, click on Message Maps [JP319].

**Figure 503 Shows that many buttons have been added to the front panel**

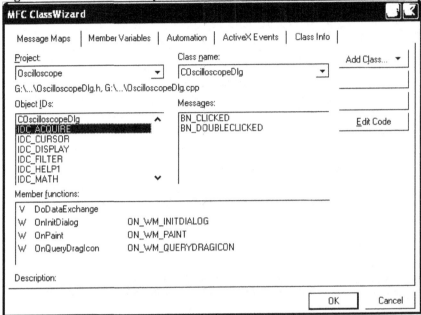

Important: Verify Project *Oscilloscope*; Class name is *COscilloscopeDlg*
In the *Object IDs* box click on push button object id *IDC_ACQUIRE*.
In the *Messages* box click *BN_CLICKED*.
This activates the *Add Function* button.
Click on *Add Function* to get *Add Member function* box. Accept *Member function* name *OnAcquire*. Click on OK. This adds code items 1, 2, 3.

1) to *OscilloscopeDlg.h* a prototype function *afx_msg void OnAcquire();*

2) to the message map in *OscilloscopeDlg.cpp* the function
*ON_BN_CLICKED(IDC_ACQUIRE, OnAcquire)*

3) in *OscilloscopeDlg.cpp* a skeleton message handler
*void COscilloscopeDlg::OnAcquire( )*

# 5 Oscilloscope Front Panel Project

After 8 menu and 4 signal push button additions
1) 12 buttons to the front panel

2) 12 prototypes to *OscilloscopeDlg.h*
```
afx_msg void OnAcquire();
afx_msg void OnCursor();
afx_msg void OnDisplay();
afx_msg void OnFilter();
afx_msg void OnMath();
afx_msg void OnMeasure();
afx_msg void OnSaveload();
afx_msg void OnUtility();

afx_msg void OnSingle();
afx_msg void OnRun();
afx_msg void OnStop();
afx_msg void OnHelp1();       // Add the 1 to avoid conflict with VisualHELP
```

3) 12 functions to the message map in *OscilloscopeDlg.cpp*.
```
ON_BN_CLICKED(IDC_ACQUIRE, OnAcquire)
ON_BN_CLICKED(IDC_CURSOR, OnCursor)
ON_BN_CLICKED(IDC_DISPLAY, OnDisplay)
ON_BN_CLICKED(IDC_FILTER, OnFilter)
ON_BN_CLICKED(IDC_MATH, OnMath)
ON_BN_CLICKED(IDC_MEASURE, OnMeasure)
ON_BN_CLICKED(IDC_SAVELOAD, OnSaveload)
ON_BN_CLICKED(IDC_UTILITY, OnUtility)

ON_BN_CLICKED(IDC_SINGLE, OnSingle)
ON_BN_CLICKED(IDC_RUN, OnRun)
ON_BN_CLICKED(IDC_STOP, OnStop)
ON_BN_CLICKED(IDC_HELP1, OnHelp1)
```

4) 12 skeleton message handlers to *OscilloscopeDlg.cpp*
```
void COscilloscopeDlg::OnAcquire()
void COscilloscopeDlg::OnCursor()
void COscilloscopeDlg::OnDisplay()
void COscilloscopeDlg::OnFilter()
void COscilloscopeDlg::OnHelp1()
void COscilloscopeDlg::OnMath()
void COscilloscopeDlg::OnMeasure()
void COscilloscopeDlg::OnSaveload()

void COscilloscopeDlg::OnSingle()
void COscilloscopeDlg::OnRun()
void COscilloscopeDlg::OnStop()
void COscilloscopeDlg::OnUtility()
```

# Programming with MFC

> Action - Add 6 vertical channel and 3 trigger push buttons. *AC1, DC1, GND1, AC2, DC2, GND2, Norm, Auto, View* (Figure 509, page 48).
>
> Then add their message handlers (see page 50)

To add buttons copy the process pages 49 and 50.

After 9 push button additions
1) 9 push buttons to the front panel

2) 9 prototypes to *OscilloscopeDlg.h*
   afx_msg void OnAc1();
   afx_msg void OnDc1();
   afx_msg void OnGnd1();

   afx_msg void OnAc2();
   afx_msg void OnDc2();
   afx_msg void OnGnd2();

   afx_msg void OnNorm();
   afx_msg void OnAuto();
   afx_msg void OnView();

3) 9 functions to the message map in *OscilloscopeDlg.cpp*.
   ON_BN_CLICKED(IDC_AC1, OnAc1)
   ON_BN_CLICKED(IDC_DC1, OnDc1)
   ON_BN_CLICKED(IDC_GND1, OnGnd1)

   ON_BN_CLICKED(IDC_AC2, OnAc2)
   ON_BN_CLICKED(IDC_DC2, OnDc2)
   ON_BN_CLICKED(IDC_GND2, OnGnd2)

   ON_BN_CLICKED(IDC_NORM, OnNorm)
   ON_BN_CLICKED(IDC_AUTO, OnAuto)
   ON_BN_CLICKED(IDC_VIEW, OnView)

4) 9 skeleton message handlers to *OscilloscopeDlg.cpp*
   void COscilloscopeDlg::OnAc1()
   void COscilloscopeDlg::OnDc1()
   void COscilloscopeDlg::OnGnd1()

   void COscilloscopeDlg::OnAc2()
   void COscilloscopeDlg::OnDc2()
   void COscilloscopeDlg::OnGnd2()

   void COscilloscopeDlg::OnNorm()
   void COscilloscopeDlg::OnAuto()
   void COscilloscopeDlg::OnView()

# 5 Oscilloscope Front Panel Project

> Action – Add static text *Menus, Signal, Vertical Channel1, Pos, Vertical Channel 2, Pos,*

*Add a static text controls that labels the menu and signal buttons*[JP331]
Drag a static text from the control tool box onto the front panel
Position the static text above coordinates x=30, y=370 (Figure 509).
Right click on the button.
Click on *Properties*.
Click on the *General* tab.
    In the *ID* edit box change nothing.
    In the *Caption* edit box type *Menus*.
    Only the boxes *Visible* and *Group* should be checked.
    Click on the X to close the *Text Properties* box.
Repeat for signal and the vertical channels


Code for Push Button Message Handlers

Add push button code to *OscilloscopeDlg.cpp*.
*Vertical channels* AC1, DC1, GND1, AC2, DC2, GND2,
*Signal* SINGLE, RUN, STOP, HELP
*Trigger* NORM, AUTO, VIEW
The 6+4+3 = 13 push buttons have message handler Code 501.

> Action - Add push button Code 501 to the *AC1( )* message handler. Repeat for 8+4+9=21 push buttons.

**Code 501 Code for all push button message handlers – add by hand**

```
void COscilloscopeDlg::OnAc1()
{
  // send "AC1 button pressed" to hardware
  AfxMessageBox("AC1 pressed", MB_OK);        // message to output
}
```

The message box output temporarily replaces a message to the USB hardware.

53

Programming with MFC

## 5.5 Code for Adding a Combo Box

*Add a Control - Combo Box Example: (JP358)*
Drag a combo box from the control tool box to the front panel
Position the combo box as the Trigger Source (Figures 501, 509, pages 47. 48).
Right click on the Combo Box.
Click on *Properties*.

**Figure 504**

Click on the *General* tab (Figure 504).
  In the *ID* edit box erase IDC_COMBO1. Type IDC_TRIGSOURCE
  Only check the boxes *Visible* and *Tab Stop*.
Click on the *Data* tab. Type in four *listbox* items on four lines.
  Channel 1 AC, Channel 1 DC, Channel 2 AC, Channel 2 DC
  (use Ctrl-Enter to start a new line)
Click on the *Styles* tab.
  In *Type* box select *DropList*,
  In *Owner draw* box select *No*,
  Check the box *Vertical scroll*. Uncheck *Sort*
  Extended Styles – no selections
Click on the X to close the *Combo Box Properties* box.

On the front panel click on the combo box's *down arrow* at the right. Pull down the bottom edge of the outline until the height is doubled. Do this in order to show all listed items after a build. Build to see if pull down was adequate. Modify accordingly.

> Action - Add 4 more combo boxes (Figure 509). Add
> IDC names, Data, and list box contents ((page 56).

54

5 Oscilloscope Front Panel Project

Click on View, click on Class Wizard, click on Message Maps [JP358].

**Figure 505 Shows that combo boxes have been added to the front panel**

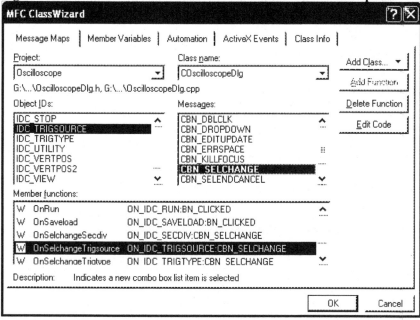

Important: Verify Project is *Oscilloscope*, Class is *COscilloscopeDlg*.
In the *Object IDs* box click on object id *IDC_TRIGSOURCE*.
In the *Messages* box select *CBN_SELCHANGE*.
This activates the *Add Function* button.

Click on *Add Function* to get *Add Member function* box. Accept *Member function* name *OnSelchangeTrigsource*.
Click on OK. This adds code items 1, 2, 3.
1) to *OscilloscopeDlg.h* a prototype function
   *afx_msg void OnSelchangeTrigsource( );*
2) to the message and data maps in *OscilloscopeDlg.cpp* the function
   ON_CBN_SELCHANGE(IDC_TRIGSOURCE, OnSelchangeTrigsource)
3) in *OscilloscopeDlg.cpp* a skeleton message handler
   *voidCOscilloscopeDlg::OnSelchangeTrigsource( )*

Action – Add 4 Combo Box Message Handlers for Message Passing

55

# Programming with MFC

> Add static text *Trigger Source, Trigger Type, Seconds/Division, Volts/division, Volts/Division* (Figure 501)

After 5 Combo box additions
1) 5 combo boxes to the front panel

2) 5 prototypes to *OscilloscopeDlg.h*
   afx_msg void OnSelchangeVoltsdiv1();
   afx_msg void OnSelchangeVoltsdiv2();
   afx_msg void OnSelchangeSecdiv();
   afx_msg void OnSelchangeTrigsource();
   afx_msg void OnSelchangeTrigtype();

3) 5 functions to the message map in *OscilloscopeDlg.cpp*.
   ON_CBN_SELCHANGE(IDC_VOLTSDIV1, OnSelchangeVoltsdiv1)
   ON_CBN_SELCHANGE(IDC_VOLTSDIV2, OnSelchangeVoltsdiv2)
   ON_CBN_SELCHANGE(IDC_SECDIV, OnSelchangeSecdiv)
   ON_CBN_SELCHANGE(IDC_TRIGSOURCE, OnSelchangeTrigsource)
   ON_CBN_SELCHANGE(IDC_TRIGTYPE, OnSelchangeTrigtype)

4) 5 skeleton message handlers to *OscilloscopeDlg.cpp*
   void COscilloscopeDlg::OnSelchangeVoltsdiv1()
   void COscilloscopeDlg::OnSelchangeVoltsdiv2()
   void COscilloscopeDlg::OnSelchangeSecdiv()
   void COscilloscopeDlg::OnSelchangeTrigsource()
   void COscilloscopeDlg::OnSelchangeTrigtype()

**Click on the *Data* tab for each combo box (done on page 54)**
Type in *listbox* items as follows (use CTRL-ENTER to start a new line).

TRIGSOURCE
*Channel 1 AC, Channel 1 DC, Channel 2 AC, Channel 2 DC*

TRIGTYPE *Edge rise, Edge fall, Pulse normal, Pulse inverted*

SECDIV     2, 5, 10, 20, 50, 100, 200, 500 ns per division
                1, 2, 5, 10, 20, 50, 100, 200, 500 micro s per division
                1, 2, 5, 10, 20, 50, 100, 200, 500 ms per division
                1, 2, 5, 10 s per division

VOLTSDIV1 and VOLTSDIV2
                2, 5, 10, 20, 50, 100, 200, 500 mv per division
                1, 2, 5, 10, 20, 50 volts per division.

# 5 Oscilloscope Front Panel Project

> Action – Add Code 502 Combo Box Variables, which add DDX to *OscilloscopeDlg* [JP402, JP404]

**Code 502 Combo Box Variables added via ClassWizard (see page 63)**

CComboBox m_wndCBvoltsdiv2;     CComboBox m_wndCBvoltsdiv1;
CComboBox m_wndCBsecdiv;         CComboBox m_wndCBtrigtype;
CComboBox m_wndCBtrigsource;

> Add *public* string variables Code 503 to *OscilloscopeDlg.h* .

**Code 503 Combo Box String Variables – add by hand**

CString m_strVoltsdiv1;   CString m_strVoltsdiv2;   CString m_strTrigsource;
CString m_strTrigtype;    CString m_strSecDiv;

> Action - Add Combo Box Handler Code 504 to 5 Combo box handlers in *OscilloscopeDlg.cpp*. Change variable names per codes 502, 503

**Code 504 Combo box message handler – add by hand**

```
void COscilloscopeDlg::OnSelchangeVoltsdiv1 ()      // (JP329, 357)
{
    int nIndex = m_wndCBvoltsdiv1.GetCurSel ();
    if (nIndex != CB_ERR) {
      m_wndCBvoltsdiv1.GetLBText(nIndex, m_strVoltsdiv1);
    }
    AfxMessageBox (m_strVoltsdiv1, MB_OK); // temporary code
}
```

**Code 504** The items in a combo box list are numbered 1, 2, 3, etc. MFC function *GetCurSel()* fetches the integer number of the currently selected item in the combo box list. *GetCurSel()* stores (returns) the number in MFC *int* variable *nIndex*. *CB_ERR* is returned if there are no items in the box. The integer index is stored in *nIndex*.

MFC function *GetLBText* uses nIndex to store in string variable *m_strVoltsdiv1* the selected volts/div item such as 50mv. *m_wndCBvoltsdiv1* is a CComboBox variable, which means it can use *CComboBox::GetCurSel* &*CComboBox::GetLBText* member functions.

Programming with MFC

## 5.6 Code for Adding a Slider

The ResourceView control tool box has a horizontal "slider". However you can select a vertical slider in the Styles tab (Figure 506). Sliders (aka TrackBars) are not fully explained in JP932 (see our Chapter 8).

*Add a Control - Slider Example: (JP932)*
  Drag a slider from the control tool box to the front panel
  Position the slider at Vertical Channel 1 Pos.
  (Figures 501, 509, pages 47. 48).
  Right click on the slider.
  Click on *Properties*.

**Figure 506 Selecting a Vertical Slider**

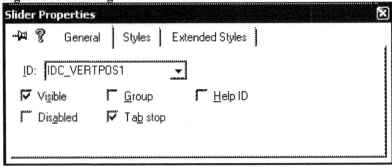

Click on the *General* tab.
  In the *ID* edit box erase IDC_SLIDER1. Type IDC_VERTPOS1
  Only check the boxes *Visible* and *Tab Stop*.
Click on the *Styles* tab.
  In *Orientation* box select- *Vertical*.
  In *Point* box select *Top/Left*.
    (the thumb pointer is at the top and points left)
  Check the boxes *Tick marks, Auto ticks*
Click on the *Extended Styles* tab
  Check *Modal frame*.
Click on the X to close the *Slider Properties* box.
In the Oscilloscope dialog box (the front panel) the slider is horizontal. Drag edges to make it vertical by reducing width and increasing height.

> Action - Add 3 sliders per Figs 501, 509.
> Add *IDC_VERTPOS2, IDC_HORZPOS, IDC_TRIGLEVEL*.

# 5 Oscilloscope Front Panel Project

*HSCROLL* and *VSCROLL* are the de facto message handlers for sliders.

> Action - Add Slider Handlers for Message Passing

Click on View, click on Class Wizard, click on Message Maps [JP932].

**Figure 507 Shows that WM_HSCROLL message has been added**

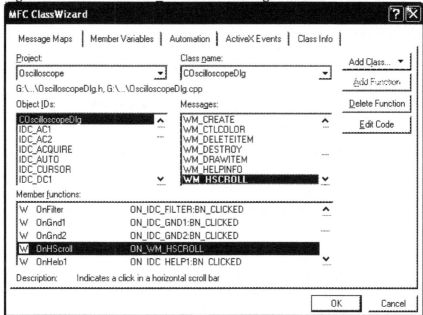

Important: Verify Project is *Oscilloscope*, Class is *COscilloscopeDlg*.
In the *Object IDs* box click on *COscilloscopeDlg*
In the *Messages* box click *WM_HSCROLL*
This activates the *Add Function* button.
Click on *Add Function* to get *Add Member function* box. Accept *Member function* name *OnHScroll*. Click on OK.
This adds code items 1, 2, 3.
1) to *OscilloscopeDlg.h* a prototype function
*afx_msg void OnHScroll(UINT nSBCode, UINT nPos, CScrollBar* pScrollBar);*
2) to the message map in *OscilloscopeDlg.cpp* the function
    ON_WM_HSCROLL()
3) in *OscilloscopeDlg.cpp* a skeleton message handler
*void COscilloscopeDlg::OnHScroll(UINT nSBCode, UINT nPos, CScrollBar* pScrollBar)*

> Action - Repeat for *VScroll*

Programming with MFC

> Action – Add Code 505 Slider Variables which add DDX to *OscilloscopeDlg* [JP402, JP404]

**Code 505 Slider Variables added via ClassWizard (see page 63)**

```
CSliderCtrl m_wndSvpos1;
CSliderCtrl m_wndSvpos2;
CSliderCtrl m_wndStriglevel;
CSliderCtrl m_wndShorzpos;
```

> Action - Add *public* variables Code 506 to *OscilloscopeDlg.h* .

**Code 506 Slider Prototype and String Variables – add by hand**

```
void InitSliders ();
CString m_strVpos1;
CString m_strVpos2;
CString m_strTriglevel;
CString m_strHorzpos;
```

Initialize each slider's range, thumb position, and tic marks.

**Code 507 Add by hand to COscilloscopeDlg::OnInitDialog().**

```
// Initialize Sliders
m_wndSvpos1.SetRange (0, 80); // draws tick marks at start and end of range
m_wndSvpos1.SetPos (10); // positions thumb at mark 10
m_wndSvpos1.SetTicFreq (10); // shows tick marks at 0, 10, 20, ... 70, 80
m_wndSvpos2.SetRange (0, 80);
m_wndSvpos2.SetPos (20);
m_wndSvpos2.SetTicFreq (10);
m_wndShorzpos.SetRange (0, 50); // Sets slider min and max position
m_wndShorzpos.SetPos (5); // Sets current position of the slider thumb
m_wndShorzpos.SetTicFreq (5); // Sets tick marks units separation
m_wndStriglevel.SetRange (0, 50);
m_wndStriglevel.SetPos (15);
m_wndStriglevel.SetTicFreq (5);
```

A range of 50 will have 1+10 tic marks when set tic freq = 5.

# 5 Oscilloscope Front Panel Project

## Sliders message handlers

When a slider thumb is moved, or clicked on, the slider sends the messages *WM_VSCROLL* or *WM_HSCROLL*.

**Code 508 Add OnHScroll to *OscilloscopeDlg.cpp* by hand**

```
void COscilloscopeDlg::OnHScroll(UINT nSBCode, UINT nPos, CScrollBar* pScrollBar)
{
  pScrollBar->GetDlgCtrlID();
  if(nSBCode == SB_THUMBPOSITION) {
    m_strHorzpos.Format("%ld", nPos);
    AfxMessageBox (m_strHorzpos, MB_OK);   // send pos to the hardware.
    UpdateData(false);
  }
  else {CDialog::OnHScroll(nSBCode, nPos, pScrollBar);
  }

  CDialog::OnHScroll(nSBCode, nPos, pScrollBar);
}
```

SB_THUMBPOSITION is a *VScroll* and *HScroll* parameter (F1). The current position is specified by the *nPos* parameter.

Each click on or movement of a thumb on a slider sends a message to *OnHScroll* or *OnVScroll*. Clicking anywhere on a slider scale moves the thumb to that position. Clicking on the thumb, *holding the mouse button down* while moving the thumb to another position, and then releasing the mouse button produces a message.

Each movement of a thumb on any slider creates a message to *OnHScroll* or *OnVScroll*. Consequently a switch statement is required so that each slider is assigned a case.

*GetDlgCtrlID* is an MFC function.

Programming with MFC

**Code 509 Add OnVScroll by hand to *OscilloscopeDlg.cpp*.**

```cpp
void COscilloscopeDlg::OnVScroll(UINT nSBCode, UINT nPos, CScrollBar* pScrollBar)
{
  // TODO: Add your message handler code here and/or call default
    switch(pScrollBar->GetDlgCtrlID()) {
    case IDC_TRIGLEVEL:
      if(nSBCode == SB_THUMBPOSITION) {
        m_strTriglevel.Format("%ld", nPos);
        AfxMessageBox(m_strTriglevel, MB_OK);

        UpdateData(false);
      }
      else {CDialog::OnHScroll(nSBCode, nPos, pScrollBar);
      }
      break;

    case IDC_VERTPOS1:
      if(nSBCode == SB_THUMBPOSITION) {
        m_strVpos1.Format("%ld", nPos);
        AfxMessageBox(m_strVpos1, MB_OK);

        UpdateData(false);
      }
      else {CDialog::OnHScroll(nSBCode, nPos, pScrollBar);
      }
      break;

    case IDC_VERTPOS2:
      if(nSBCode == SB_THUMBPOSITION) {
        m_strVpos2.Format("%ld", nPos);
        AfxMessageBox(m_strVpos2, MB_OK);

        UpdateData(false);
      }
      else {CDialog::OnHScroll(nSBCode, nPos, pScrollBar);
      }
      break;
    }

    CDialog::OnVScroll(nSBCode, nPos, pScrollBar);
}
```

## 5.7 Code for Combo Box and Slider Variables

Member variables used in the message handlers are added via *Class Wizard* in the Member Variable tab, because this is how the DDX functions are added [JP402, JP404].

Action – Add a variable.

**Figure 508 Adding a slider variable**

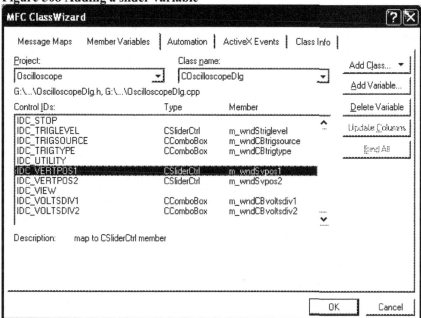

Click on View, click Class Wizard, click Member Variables tab.
Important: Check project is *Oscilloscope*, class name is *COscilloscopeDlg*
In the *Control IDs* box click on *IDC_VERTPOS1*.
Click on *Add Variable* to get *Add Member Variable* dialog box.
Enter member variable name *m_wndSvpos1*
Click on *Category*. Select *control*.
Click on OK.

This adds code items 1, 2.
1) to *OscilloscopeDlg.h* a variable *CSliderCtrl m_wndSvpos1;*

2) to *OscilloscopeDlg.cpp*
*DDX_Control(pDX, IDC_VERTPOS1, m_wndSvpos1);*

Programming with MFC

## 5.8 Code for Support functions

**Code 510 Add prototype CrtScreen to *OscilloscopeDlg.h* – add by hand**

```
void CrtScreen ();
```

**Code 511 Add Display Screen Defines to *OscilloscopeDlg.cpp* by hand**

```
//crt screen
#define u0  50
#define v0  45
#define u1  500
#define v1  333
#define HOUT 10
#define VOUT 8
```

**Code 512 Add CrtScreen to *OscilloscopeDlg.cpp* by hand**

```
void COscilloscopeDlg::CrtScreen ()      // nlp
{
  CClientDC dc(this); // device context for painting

  // select body brush color
  CBrush brush (RGB (255, 255, 230));
  CBrush* pOldBrush = dc.SelectObject (&brush);

  // create black solid pen
  CPen pen1 (PS_SOLID, 2, RGB (0, 0, 0,));  // (JP 60, 61)
  CPen* pOldPen1 = dc.SelectObject (&pen1);

  // K-Draw the body of the Output display.
  dc.Rectangle (u0, v0, u1, v1);

  // create gray solid pen   //light gray (JP 60, 61)
  CPen pen0 (PS_SOLID, 1, RGB (130, 130, 130,));
  CPen* pOldPen0 = dc.SelectObject (&pen0);

  // Draw H and V lines
  int dx=(u1 - u0)/HOUT;
  int dy=(v1 - v0)/VOUT;
  int i;
```

# 5 Oscilloscope Front Panel Project

```
   // H-Draw the Output horizontal lines.
   for (i=1; i<VOUT; i++)
   {
      dc.MoveTo(u0, v0+(dy*i));
      dc.LineTo(u1, v0+(dy*i));
   }

   // H-Draw the Output vertical lines.
   for (i=1; i<HOUT; i++)
   {
      dc.MoveTo(u0+(dx*i), v0);
      dc.LineTo(u0+(dx*i), v1);
   }

   return;
} //end of CrtScreen
```

**Code 513 Add to OnPaint in *OscilloscopeDlg.cpp* by hand**

```
void COscilloscopeDlg::OnPaint()
{
   CPaintDC dc(this); // device context for painting
   CrtScreen ();
   CDialog::OnPaint();
} //end of OnPaint
```

Programming with MFC

## 5.9 A Simple Help Program

This is the simple help system. The Help push button was installed on page 50.

**Code 514 Add OnHelp1() to *OscilloscopeDlg.cpp*. by hand**

```
void COscilloscopeDlg::OnHelp1()
{
    // TODO: Add your control notification handler code here
    CString strRightClick ;
    strRightClick = (CString)              // casts text into a string
    "Set up a vertical channel input by selecting AC, DC , or GND."
    + "\n"
    + " Use Pos to set up a vertical channel zero signal line on the screen."
    + "\n"
    + "Select Volts/Div vertical scale for each channel."
    + "\n"
    + "Select the Trigger Source."
    + "\n"
    + "Select the Trigger Type."
    + "\n"
    + "Set the trigger Level and select Norm, Auto, or View trigger format."
    + "\n"
    + "Select Seconds/Division for the horizontal sweep speed."
    + "\n"
    + "Use Horizontal Position to adjust sweep position after a signal appears."
    + "\n"
    + "The Menus show features available for oscilloscope operation."
    + "\n"
    + "Select Controls – single sweep, run continuously, stop, or get help."
    ;
    MessageBox(strRightClick,"Help", MB_OK);      // (JP116)
}
```

# 6 Design a Property Sheet connected to a Menu Button

A property sheet is convenient to include in a program, because the property sheet is an assembly of pages, and each page is a dialog box to which as many controls one desires can be added.

This design project shows how to create a property sheet with four property pages (JP449) that is accessed via a button in the File menu.

The four property pages are dialog boxes. Important: The property sheet **is not a dialog box** (Section 6.5 page 70).

## 6.1 Create the *PropSheetMenu* Workspace

Follow the procedure in Chapter 1, Section 1.1 page 1 for *Single Document* except as follows.
    Type the name *PropSheetMenu* in the *Project Name* edit box.
    Note addition of *PropSheetMenu* in the *Location* edit box.

## 6.2 Build the *PropSheetMenu* Project and Change Title

Follow the procedure in Chapter 1, Section 1.4 page 4.
Follow the procedure in Chapter 1, Section 1.5 page 5.

**Figure 601 The main window showing the rectangle**

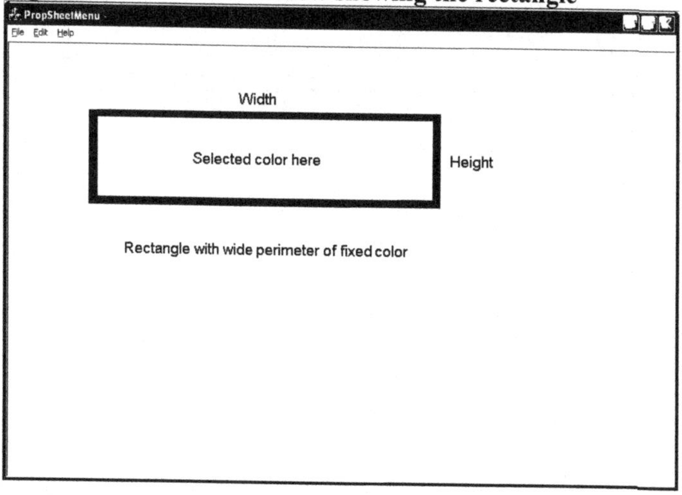

Programming with MFC

## 6.3 Use *ResourceView* to create four Property Page Dialog Boxes

For each page in the property sheet, create a dialog template (box) here to which controls are added in Section 6.6 [JP449 item 1]

1 Click ResourceView Tab in left pane.
  Click + to left of *PropSheetMenu Resources*.
  Click + to left of *Dialog*. See IDD_ABOUTBOX

2 Click *Insert* in menu bar at top of screen, Click *Resource*
  Click on + next to *Dialog* in the *Insert Resource* dialog box.
  Click on *IDD_Proppage_Large*
  Click on *New*.
IDD_PROPPAGE_LARGE appears in the left pane, and the *Property Page* dialog box appears in right pane.

3 Right click in the *Property Page* dialog box. Click on *Properties* to get the *Dialog Properties* box (Figure 602.

**Figure 602 Page 1 Properties**

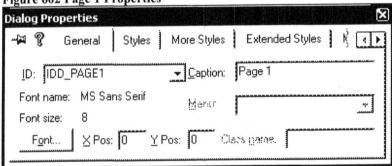

  Change ID box IDD_PROPPAGE_LARGE to IDD_PAGE1
  Change caption box to *Page 1*.
  Do not change anything else.
  Click on X. IDD_PAGE1 appears in the left pane.
  Dialog box title is now *Page 1*
  Delete the text box on the page.

4 Repeat 2 and 3 with IDD_PAGE2 and *Page 2*.

5 Repeat 2 and 3 with IDD_PAGE3 and *Page 3*.

6 Repeat 2 and 3 with IDD_PAGE4 and *Page 4*.

# 6 Design a Property Sheet

## 6.4 Use *ClassWizard* to create four pairs of Property Page Files

For each page in the property sheet, construct here a page class to which public data member variables are added in Section 6.6 [JP449 item 2].

1 In the *ResourceView* Pane, click on +PropSheetMenu resources, click on +Dialog.

2 Click on IDD_PAGE1

3 In the *View* menu click *ClassWizard* to open *MFC ClassWizard*. Select the *Message Maps* tab. The *Adding a Class* dialog *box* appears.

4 Click OK in the *Adding a Class* dialog *box*.
  Type *CPage1* in the Name edit box
  Select *CPropertyPage* in the Base Class edit box.
  Verify that the Dialog ID box contains IDD_PAGE1.
  Click on *OK*.
  Click on *OK*.
  Click on *FileView* to see new files *Page1.h* and *Page1.cpp*.

3 Click on IDD_PAGE2. Repeat 3, and 4 for *CPage2*.

4 Click on IDD_PAGE3. Repeat 3, and 4 for *CPage3*.

5 Click on IDD_PAGE4. Repeat 3, and 4 for *CPage4*.

Programming with MFC

## 6.5 Use *ClassWizard* to create a Property Sheet

Here we create a property sheet class that instantiates the property pages, which are implemented in Section 6.6 [JP449 item 3].

1 In the *View* menu click on *ClassWizard* to open *MFC ClassWizard*.
   Select the *Message Maps* tab [JP449].
2 Click on *Add Class, then click on New* to open *New Class* dialog box.
   Type *CMyPropertySheet* in the Name edit box.
   Select *CPropertySheet* in the Base Class edit box.
   Click on *OK*. Click on *OK* to close *ClassWizard*.
   In Fileview see new files *MyPropertySheet.h* and *.cpp*.
3 In Fileview click on *MyPropertySheet.h*

**Code 601 Add Includes to *MyPropertySheet.h* after *#define afx* by hand**

*#include "Page1.h"*
*#include "Page2.h"*
*#include "Page3.h"*
*#include "Page4.h"*

**Code 602 Add variables to *MyPropertySheet.h* after // Attributes by hand**

*CPage1 m_Page1;*
*CPage2 m_Page2;*
*CPage3 m_Page3;*
*CPage4 m_Page4;*

4 In Fileview click on *MyPropertySheet.cpp*.

**Code 603 Add AddPage() by hand to the first two functions following IMPLEMENT_DYNAMIC in *MyPropertySheet.cpp*.**

*AddPage(&m_Page1);*
*AddPage(&m_Page2);*
*AddPage(&m_Page3);*
*AddPage(&m_Page4);*

5 Verify that the following code is at the top of *MyPropertySheet.cpp*
   *#include " MyPropertySheet.h"*

# 6 Design a Property Sheet

## 6.6 Add Controls to the Property Pages

Creating the property sheet with four pages is straightforward (6.3, 6.4, 6.5). Adding controls to the pages is also straightforward. However, transferring data changes in the controls to the main program is complex.

Adding controls to a property sheet page is straightforward, because each page is a dialog box (6.6.1. 6.6.2). However a difference appears, because each data change in the pages has to call *SetModified* [JP453] to enable the Apply button (6.8). The call is implemented by *OnChange*. This is why *OnChange* has to be the message handler for each control [JP453]. FYI *OnChange* is an arbitrary name.

For example change
*ON_BN_CLICKED(IDC_RED, OnRed)*       to
*ON_BN_CLICKED(IDC_RED, OnChange)*

Furthermore member variables are added to the pages via Class Wizard so that DDX functions are automatically added (e.g. Code 605 page 73).

Entering data in a control does NOT place the data in variables. The DDX functions transfer a control's data to variables [JP399].

We named the menu button *PropSheet* (6.7) Clicking on this button opens the property sheet so that a user can change data in pages 1 and 2 (Figures 603, 604, 605). A data change enables the property sheet Apply button (6.8), and clicking on the OK button implements the changes via *OnFilePropSheet*, which are then displayed on the screen.

**Figure 603 The empty Property Sheet**

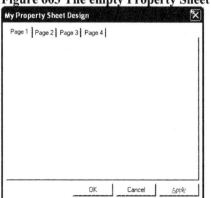

Programming with MFC

## 6.6.1 Selecting Rectangle Color (CPage2)

***Add a control – red radio button*** [JP319]
Drag a radio button from the control tool box onto *Page 2*.
Position the button as the *Red* button (Figure 604).
Right click on the button.
Click on *Properties*.
In the Radio Button Properties dialog box click on the *General* tab.
In the *ID* box erase *IDC_RADIO1*. Type *IDC_RED* .
In the *Caption* edit box type *&Red*. This is the radio button title.
Only the check boxes *Visible* and perhaps *Group* should be checked.
Note: If a button is the first button in a group, then check the group box.
Click on the X to close the *Radio Button Properties* box.

***Add the red button message handler***
Click on View, click on Class Wizard, click on Message Maps [JP319].
Verify Project is *PropSheetMenu*; Class name is *CPage2* (Figure 603).
In the *Object IDs* box click on object id *IDC_RED*.
In the *Messages* box click *BN_CLICKED*.
This activates the *Add Function* button.
Click on *Add Function* to get *Add Member function* box.
Important - Change *Member function name* to *OnChange*. Click on OK.
Click on OK.
This adds code items 1, 2, 3.
1) to *Page2.h* a prototype function *afx_msg void OnChange();*
2) to the message map in *Page2.cpp* the following function is added:
*ON_BN_CLICKED(IDC_RED, OnChange)*
3) in *Page2.cpp* a skeleton message handler *void CPage2::OnChange()*

**Figure 604 Page2**

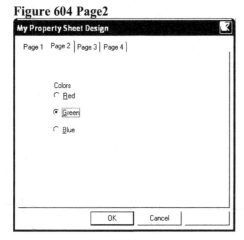

# 6 Design a Property Sheet

> Repeat for the Green and Blue radio buttons.

> Action- Add Code 604 to message handler *OnChange()* Page2.cpp

**Code 604 Add code for radio buttons to Page2.cpp *OnChange* – *use Class Wizard***

void CPage2::OnChange()  {    SetModified (TRUE);  }

> Action – Use the **Add a control** procedure to add a group box control enclosing radio buttons, *Red, Green, Blue* [JP323]. Right click on the group box and change the Caption to *Colors*. Check the Group box. Click on X.

**Code 605 Add member variable m_nColor to *Page2.h* – *use Class Wizard***

int m_nColor;    // see page 63
// this action adds a DDX function to Page2.cpp
   DDX_Radio(pDX, IDC_RED, m_nColor);
// this also initializes the variable in the Page2 constructor
   m_nColor = -1;

**Code 606 Add array definition *m_RGBColors[3]* to *Page2.h* –*by hand***

// after public    CPage2();   ~CPage2();
   static const COLORREF m_RGBColors[3];

**Code 607 Add array m_Colors[3] to *Page2.cpp* –*by hand***

// add after *OnChange( )* Function
const COLORREF CPage2::m_RGBColors[3] = {
  RGB (255,  0,  0), // Red
  RGB (  0, 255, 0), // Green
  RGB (  0,  0, 255)  // Blue
};

Programming with MFC

## 6.6.2 Selecting Rectangle Size (CPage1)

Rectangle size is defined by integer variables *m_nWidth* and *m_nHeight*. Numbers are typed in the edit boxes, and DDX functions connect the numbers typed in the edit boxes to the variables.

**Edit box [JP342]**
   Drag an edit box from the control tool box to the Page1 dialog.
   Position the edit box according to the desired Page1 design.
   Right click on the edit box.
   Click on *Properties*.
   Click on the *General* tab.
     In the *ID* edit box erase IDC_EDIT1, type IDC_EDIT_HEIGHT
     Only check the boxes *Visible* and *Tab Stop*.
   Click on the *Styles* tab.
     In *Align Text* select *Left*.
     Check boxes *Auto Scroll, No hide selection, Border*
   Click on the X to close the Box.

Action – Repeat for the Width edit box.

Action – Add static boxes next to edit boxes (Figure 605).

**Figure 605 Page1**

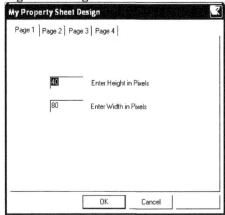

# 6 Design a Property Sheet

> Action- Add message handler *OnChange()* to Page1.cpp

Click on View, click on Class Wizard, click on Message Maps [JP319].
Verify Project is *PropSheetMenu*; Class name is *CPage1* (Figure 603).
In the *Object IDs* box click on object id *IDC_EDIT_HEIGHT*.
In the *Messages* box click *EN_CHANGE*.
This activates the *Add Function* button.
Click on *Add Function* to get *Add Member function* box.
Change *Memberfunction* name to *OnChange*. Click on OK.

This adds code items 1, 2, 3.
1) to *Page1.h* a prototype function *afx_msg void OnChange()*;

2) to the message map in *Page1.cpp* the following function is added:
*ON_EN_CHANGE(IDC_EDIT_HEIGHT, OnChange)*

3) in *Page1.cpp* a skeleton message handler *void CPage1::OnChange()*

**Code 608 Add code for edit boxes to Page1.cpp – add by hand**

```
void CPage1::OnChange()
{
   SetModified (TRUE);
}
```

> Repeat for the Width Edit box.

> Action – Add member variables (see page 63).

**Code 609 Add member variables to *Page1.h* – use Class Wizard**

```
int m_nHeight;
int m_nWidth;
// this also adds DDX functions to Page1.cpp
   DDX_Text(pDX, IDC_EDIT_WIDTH, m_nWidth);
   DDX_Text(pDX, IDC_EDIT_HEIGHT, m_nHeight);
// this also initializes the variables
   m_nWidth = 0;
   m_nHeight = 0;
```

Programming with MFC

## 6.7 PropSheet Menu Button Opens Property Sheet

Here is how this works. Clicking on the menu item (with arbitrary name) PropSheet opens the four page property sheet (with arbitrary title) My Property Sheet Design.

The property sheet is connected to a menu button in the file menu [JP449 item 4]. The code is placed in the view file so that changes can be seen.

**1)** Click *ResourceView*. Click on *+Menu*, click on *IDR_MAINFRAME*.

**2)** In the right hand pane click on *File*, right click on the *New* button
Right click on *Properties*.
change *ID_FILE_NEW* to *ID_FILE_PROPSHEET*
change the caption to *&PropSheet\tCtrl+P*. Click on X

**3)** Create a message handler for the *PropSheet* menu item.
In the *View* menu click on *ClassWizard*.
Verify that Project is *PropSheetMenu*, and class name is *CPropsheetMenuView*.
In Object ID click on *ID_FILE_PROPSHEET*
In Messages click on *COMMAND*.
Click on *Add Function* to get *Add Member function* box.
The name *OnFilePropSheet* appears in the *Add Member Functions* box.
Accept the name. Click on OK.
Click on Edit code button to go to *OnFilePropsheet* in *CPropsheetMenuView.cpp*.

Verify *ON_COMMAND(ID_FILE_PROPSHEET, OnFilePropsheet)* is in the *CPropsheetMenuView.cpp* message map.

Verify that *afx_msg void OnFilePropsheet();* is in *CPropsheetMenuView.h* message map.

> Action - Add #include "MyPropertySheet.h" at the top of *CPropsheetMenuView.cpp*.

# 6 Design a Property Sheet

**Code 610 Add variables to *CPropsheetMenuView.h* by hand**

```
// after protected
  int m_nHeight;
  int m_nWidth;
  int m_nColor;
```

**Code 611 Add OnFilePropsheet to *CPropsheetMenuView.cpp* by hand**

```
void CPropSheetMenuView::OnFilePropsheet()
{
  // Note: ps is a convenient fake word used here.
  CMyPropertySheet ps(_T("My Property Sheet Design"));
  ps.m_Page1.m_nWidth = m_nWidth;
  ps.m_Page1.m_nHeight = m_nHeight;
  ps.m_Page2.m_nColor = m_nColor;

  if (ps.DoModal () == IDOK) {
    m_nWidth = ps.m_Page1.m_nWidth;
    m_nHeight = ps.m_Page1.m_nHeight;
    m_nColor = ps.m_Page2.m_nColor;
    Invalidate ();
  }
}
```

**Code 612 Add initialized variables to *CPropsheetMenuView.cpp* by hand**

```
CPropSheetMenuView::CPropSheetMenuView()
{
  // TODO: add construction code here
  m_nHeight = 40
  m_nWidth  = 80;
  m_nColor = 1;
}
```

Programming with MFC

## 6.8 The Apply Button Transfers the Data

Here is how this works. Click on the PropSheet line in the File menu, which calls void CPropSheetMenuView::OnFilePropsheet() to create and expose the property sheet in the main window. Assume a user makes changes to data on page1 and, or page 2. Clicking on the property sheet OK button executes *OnApply*, which transfers data to the property sheet member variables (Codes 605, 609). Then *OnFilePropsheet()* transfers data from the property sheet member variables to the view member variables, which changes the display.

**Code 613 DO NOT ADD THIS CODE structure and define to StdAfx.h**

```
// WE SHOW THIS CODE, BECAUSE JP uses this – not necessary
typedef struct tagELLPROP {
    int nWidth;
    int nHeight;
    int nColor;
} ELLPROP;

#define WM_USER_APPLY WM_USER+0x100
```

**Code 614 Add prototype to MyPropertySheet.h by hand**

```
afx_msg void OnApply ();        // before  DECLARE_MESSAGE_MAP()
```

**Code 615 Add map and message handler to MyPropertySheet.cpp by hand**

```
ON_BN_CLICKED (ID_APPLY_NOW, OnApply)      // message map

void CMyPropertySheet::OnApply ()          // message handler
{
    GetActivePage ()->UpdateData (TRUE);

// JP uses ELLPROP and ep's - omit – not necessary
//     ELLPROP ep;
//     ep.nWidth = m_Page1.m_nWidth;
//     ep.nHeight = m_Page1.m_nHeight;
//     ep.m_nColor = m_Page2.m_nColor;

//     GetParent ()->SendMessage (WM_USER_APPLY, 0, (LPARAM) &ep);
    m_Page1.SetModified (FALSE);
    m_Page2.SetModified (FALSE);
}
```

# 6 Design a Property Sheet

## 6.9 Displaying a Rectangle on Screen

Drawing an object is discussed in Chapter 3. Object parameters are set by the default map mode [JP45, 46], and brush and pen functions [JP60, 64].

**Code 616 Add by a Rectangle to OnDraw in *CPropsheetMenuView.cpp*.**

```
void CPropSheetMenuView::OnDraw(CDC* pDC)
{

// CPropSheetMenuDoc* pDoc = GetDocument();
// ASSERT_VALID(pDoc);
   // TODO: add draw code for native data here
   pDC = GetDC ();   // Get Device Context

   //Brush and pen functions
   CBrush brush (CPage2::m_RGBColors[m_nColor]);
   CBrush* pOldBrush = pDC -> SelectObject (&brush);

   CPen pen (PS_SOLID,4,RGB(255,255,00));
   CPen* pOldPen = pDC -> SelectObject (&pen);

   pDC -> Rectangle (100, 80, 100+m_nWidth, 80+m_nHeight);
}
```

# 7 More About Sliders

This design project shows how to connect a slider to an edit box that displays the slider's position (JP933), and shows how to write code when there is more than one slider in the same dialog box.

## 7.1 Create a Dialog Based Project Workspace

Follow the procedure in Chapter 1, Section 1.3 Dialog Based except as follows.
    Type the name *Slider* in the *Project Name* edit box.
    Note addition of *Slider* in the *Location* edit box.
    In step 2 of 4 screen type the title *Slider Example*.

## 7.2 Build the *Slider* Project

Follow the procedure in Chapter 1, Section 1.4
Follow the procedure in Chapter 1, Section 1.5

Note: After adding code to any file repeat 7.2 to check for errors.

7 More About Sliders

**Figure 701 Slider Project**

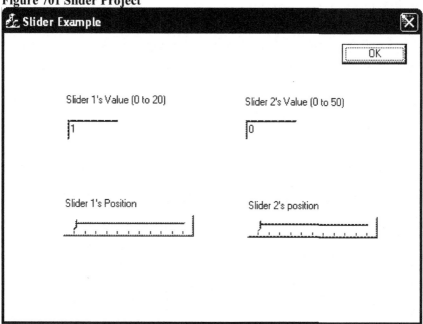

**Figure 702 Slider Dialog Control Positions**

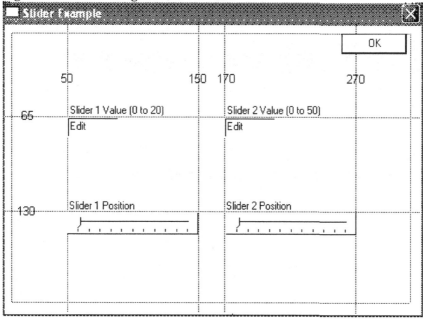

Programming with MFC

## 7.3 Add Controls to Slider Example Dialog Box

1) Click on the *Cancel* button. Right click, select cut to remove button
Click on the *text box*. Right click, select cut to remove the text.

2) Drag four static texts from the control tool box to the dialog box. Position them per Figure 702. Right click on each static text box, and in the Caption box type the text per Figure 702.

3) Drag two edit boxes from the control tool box to the dialog box. Position them per Figure 702. Right click on each edit box, and in the Properties ID boxes type IDC_SLIDER_VALUE1 and VALUE2.

4) Drag two slider controls from the control tool box to the dialog box. Position them per Figure 702. Right click on the slider 1 control, click on Properties, and accept the ID IDC_SLIDER1. In the Styles Tab select *Bottom/right* for *Point*. Check *Tick Marks* and *Auto Ticks*. In the Extended Styles Tab check *Modal Frame*. Repeat with IDC_SLIDER2.

5) Right-click in dialog box and select ClassWizard (Figure 703).
Member variables used in the message handlers are added via *Class Wizard* in the Member Variables tab.

**Figure 703 Adding Member Variables**

| Control IDs | Type | Member |
|---|---|---|
| IDC_SLIDER_VALUE1 | CString | m_SliderValue1 |
| IDC_SLIDER_VALUE2 | CString | m_SliderValue2 |
| IDC_SLIDER1 | CSliderCtrl | m_Slider1 |
| IDC_SLIDER2 | CSliderCtrl | m_Slider2 |
| IDOK | | |

Description: map to CSliderCtrl member

# 7 More About Sliders

6) Click Member Variables tab.
Important: Check project is *Slider*, class name is *CSliderDlg*
In the *Controlt IDs* box click on *IDC_SLIDER1*.
  Click on *Add Variable* to get *Add Member Variable* dialog box.
  Enter member variable name *m_Slider1*
  Click on *Category*. Select *Control*. Note: *Variable type is CSliderCtrl*.
  Click on OK. Click on OK.
  Repeat for variable *m_Slider2*
Check that the above adds code items a and b.
a) to *sliderDlg.h* under Dialog Data
  *CSliderCtrl m_Slider1;* and *CSliderCtrl m_Slider2;*
b) to *sliderDlg.cpp*
  *DDX_Control(pDX, IDC_SLIDER2, m_Slider2);*
  *DDX_Control(pDX, IDC_SLIDER1, m_Slider1);*

7) Add member variables *m_SliderValue1, m_SliderValue2*.
Click on *Category*. Select *Value*. For variable type select *CString*.

8) Open the MFC ClassWizard dialog box, and click Message Maps.
In the Object IDs list box, click *CSliderDlg*. In the list of Member Functions, click WM_INITDIALOG. Click the *Edit Code* button.

> Add Code 701 to *OnInitDialog* after the *TODO* line.

**Code 701 The slider control parameters – add by hand**

```
m_Slider1.SetRange(0,20);
m_Slider1.SetTicFreq (2);
m_SliderValue1 = "1";
UpdateData(FALSE);

m_Slider2.SetRange(0,50);
m_Slider2.SetTicFreq (5);
m_SliderValue2 = "0";
UpdateData(FALSE);
```

9) As explained on page 59, sliders communicate via HScroll and VScroll. Code 702 reads slider positions into the slider value variables. In the Object IDs list box, click *CSliderDlg*. In the list of Messages, click *WM_HSCROLL*. Click *Edit Code*. Add the *OnHScroll* code 702.

Programming with MFC

### Code 702 Add OnHScroll to SliderDlg.cpp by hand

```
void CSliderDlg::OnHScroll(UINT nSBCode, UINT nPos, CScrollBar* pScrollBar)
{
  // TODO: Add your message handler code here and/or call default
    switch(pScrollBar ->GetDlgCtrlID()) {
    case IDC_SLIDER1:
        if(nSBCode == SB_THUMBPOSITION) {
          m_SliderValue1.Format("%ld", nPos);
          UpdateData(false);
        }
        else {CDialog::OnHScroll(nSBCode, nPos, pScrollBar);
        }
        break;

    case IDC_SLIDER2:
        if(nSBCode == SB_THUMBPOSITION) {
          m_SliderValue2.Format("%ld", nPos);
          UpdateData(false);
        }
        else {CDialog::OnHScroll(nSBCode, nPos, pScrollBar);
        }
        break;
    }
}
```

10) The code that connects slider position to the edit boxes are the DDX functions (JP397). DDX functions map control data to member variables. Class Wizard automatically installs DDX functions (steps 6 and 7). Here is code copied from SliderDlg.cpp

```
void CSliderDlg::DoDataExchange(CDataExchange* pDX)
{
  CDialog::DoDataExchange(pDX);
  //{{AFX_DATA_MAP(CSliderDlg)
  DDX_Control(pDX, IDC_SLIDER2, m_Slider2);
  DDX_Control(pDX, IDC_SLIDER1, m_Slider1);
  DDX_Text(pDX, IDC_SLIDER_VALUE1, m_SliderValue1);
  DDX_Text(pDX, IDC_SLIDER_VALUE2, m_SliderValue2);
  //}}AFX_DATA_MAP
}
```

# 8 Tic Tac Toe - a Document/View Project

The goal here is to understand the *document/view* architecture. We recast JP's Tic Tac program [JP106] as a *single document/view* project named *TicTacToe* by using AppWizard and ClassWizard.

The Tic Tac Toe game board consists of a 3 x 3 array of squares (Figure 801). One player writes X's in the squares. A second player writes O's in the squares. The program guarantees players take turns. After each X or O is placed the game checks for a winner or a draw. A winner has placed three X's, or O's, in a horizontal row, a vertical row, or a diagonal. A draw occurs when 9 squares are filled and there is no winner.

Clicking the left mouse button over an empty square places an X in the square. Clicking the right mouse button over an empty square places an O in the square.

Double clicking the left mouse button over any grid line clears the board, and starts a new game, or click on *Reset* in the *File* menu.

**Figure 801 Tic Tac Toe Window**

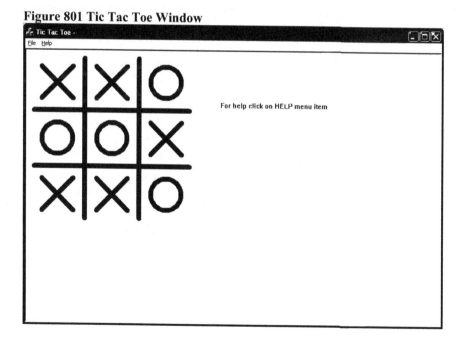

Programming with MFC

## 8.1 Create the *TicTacToe* project Workspace

Follow the procedure in Chapter 1, Section 1.1 for a single document project.
    Type the name *TicTacToe* in the *Project Name* edit box.
    Note addition of *TicTacToe* in the *Location* edit box.

This is different - in Step 4 click the *Advance* button. Type *tic* in the File Extension box. This defines the file name extension for files in this project.

## 8.2 Build and Execute the *TicTacToe* Project

Follow the procedures in Chapter 1, Sections 1.4, 1.5.

## 8.3 Code for Document Functions

Document code is placed in *TicTacToeDoc.h* and *TicTacToeDoc.cpp*.

**Code 801 Add data prototypes and data variables to *TicTacToeDoc.h* under // *Operations* – add by hand**

```
void CheckForGameOver ();
int GetRectID (CPoint point);
int IsWinner ();
BOOL IsDraw ();
void ResetGame ();

int m_nGameGrid[9];   // the data -- X and O in the grid
int m_nNextChar;      // X or O is next (EX or OH)
static const CRect m_rcSquares[9];   // size and position of board squares
```

In effect we are replacing JP's *CMainwindow* with *CTicTacToeDoc*.

## 8 Tic Tac Toe - a Document/View Project

**Code 802 Add Define after *#endif*, to the *TicTacToeDoc.cpp* – add by hand**

*#define EX 1*
*#define OH 2*

Add **by hand** ALL of the following data functions to *TicTacToeDoc.cpp*

**Code 803 IsWinner**

```
int CTicTacToeDoc::IsWinner ()
{
   static int nPattern[8][3] = {
      0, 1, 2,
      3, 4, 5,
      6, 7, 8,
      0, 3, 6,
      1, 4, 7,
      2, 5, 8,
      0, 4, 8,
      2, 4, 6
   };

   for (int i=0; i<8; i++) {
      if ((m_nGameGrid[nPattern[i][0]] == EX) &&
          (m_nGameGrid[nPattern[i][1]] == EX) &&
          (m_nGameGrid[nPattern[i][2]] == EX))
         return EX;

      if ((m_nGameGrid[nPattern[i][0]] == OH) &&
          (m_nGameGrid[nPattern[i][1]] == OH) &&
          (m_nGameGrid[nPattern[i][2]] == OH))
         return OH;
   }
   return 0;
}
```

Programming with MFC

**Array** The general form of a single dimension array is *type name[size]*. The *static* modifier, as in *static type name[size]*, creates permanent storage for the array. This means the array contents are preserved between function calls. The contents are always available.

**Static** *static int nPattern[8][3]* is declared here. It is a two dimensional array of 24 numbers arranged as 8 rows of 3 numbers per row, which are initalized as shown. Each array row represents a winner of 3 X's or 3 O's. Each array element is the number of a board square. The numbers 0 to 8 are the numbers of the 9 squares in the Tic Tac Toe game board.

**Reading arrays** The array *nPattern[ ]* stores winner sequences of X's and O's. For example the 3 square numbers 2, 4, 6 in *nPattern[ ]* row 7 represents a winner, because squares 2, 4, 6 are a diagonal of board squares.

If a player marks squares 2, 4, 6 with an X, then *m_nGameGrid* elements 2, 4, 6 are set to 1. {The array *m_nGameGrid[9]* stores the X's and O's selected by the players.) Ascertaining whether or not there is a winner requires reading arrays *nPattern* and *m_nGameGrid*.

**For loops** The for loop in code 803 repeatedly reads out the values of sequences of 3 elements of array *m_nGameGrid*, and AND's the 3 values. If the AND = 1, then 3 X's or 3 O's is a winner. Each sequence is determined by the elements in a row of array *nPattern*.

The elements of *m_nGameGrid* were set to zero by the function *OnNewDocument* (page 91). Therefore an element equal to zero means a player did NOT place an X or O in the corresponding square. In turn this means the game is not over, and function *IsDraw* returns a FALSE on exit.

The game is indeed over if no element equals zero, because that means 9 X's and O's have been played. Then the *IsDraw if* statement does not execute, and instead *return TRUE* executes.

In code 806: *IsWinner ()* returns an EX if X wins, an OH if O wins, or a zero if neither player wins. Consequently the *if* expression (*nWinner = IsWinner ()*) assigns an EX, OH, or zero to variable nWinner.

# 8 Tic Tac Toe - a Document/View Project

**Code 804 IsDraw**

```
BOOL CTicTacToeDoc::IsDraw ()
{
   for (int i=0; i<9; i++) {
     if (m_nGameGrid[i] == 0)
        return FALSE;
   }
   return TRUE;
}
```

**Code 805 ResetGame**

```
void CTicTacToeDoc::ResetGame ()
{
   m_nNextChar = EX;
   ::ZeroMemory (m_nGameGrid, 9 * sizeof (int));
}
```

*ResetGame* zeros the elements of array *m_nGameGrid*. To know why see function *IsDraw* above. *ZeroMemory* is an MFC function.

**Code 806 CheckForGameOver**

```
// If the grid contains 3 consecutive Xs or Os, declare a winner & Start a new
// game.
// Else if the grid is full, declare a draw and start a new game.

void CTicTacToeDoc::CheckForGameOver ()
{
   int nWinner;
   if (nWinner = IsWinner ()) {
     CString string = (nWinner == EX)
                  ? _T ("X wins! Game Over") : _T ("O wins! Game Over");
     AfxMessageBox (string, MB_ICONEXCLAMATION | MB_OK, 0);
     ResetGame ();
   }
   else if (IsDraw ()) {
     AfxMessageBox
     (_T ("It's a draw! Game Over"), MB_ICONEXCLAMATION | MB_OK, 0);
     ResetGame ();
   }
}
```

Programming with MFC

**Variable** *CString string* is assigned the 0 or 1 stored in *nWinner*.

**? operator** The ? operator takes the general form *Exp1 ? Exp2 : Exp3*. If Exp1 is true, then Exp2 is evaluated. If Exp1 is false, then Exp3 is evaluated.
*Exp1* is *CString string = (nWinner == EX)*, which evaluates to 0 or 1.

**Code 807 Define the board squares.**

```
const CRect CTicTacToeDoc::m_rcSquares[9] = {
    CRect ( 16,  16, 112, 112),
    CRect (128,  16, 224, 112),
    CRect (240,  16, 336, 112),
    CRect ( 16, 128, 112, 224),
    CRect (128, 128, 224, 224),
    CRect (240, 128, 336, 224),
    CRect ( 16, 240, 112, 336),
    CRect (128, 240, 224, 336),
    CRect (240, 240, 336, 336)
};
```

Define the board squares as 9 rectangles in array *m_rcSquares[9]*.

**Code 808 GetRectID**

```
// Test each of the grid's nine squares for an X or O, and return a rectangle
// integer ID (0 to 8) if  mouse (point.x, point.y) lies inside a square (rectangle)

int CTicTacToeDoc::GetRectID (CPoint point)
{
   for (int i=0; i<9; i++) {
     if (m_rcSquares[i].PtInRect (point))
        return i;
   }
   return –1;
}
```

*CRect::PtInRect* is an MFC member function of class *CRect*.

Function *BOOL PtInRect( POINT point ) const* return value is nonzero if the point lies within any board array square, otherwise return value is **0**.

Array *m_rcSquares[9]* is defined as *static const CRect m_rcSquares[9]*.

# 8 Tic Tac Toe - a Document/View Project

Therefore *m_rcSquares[9]* can *dot* execute the *CRECT* member function *PtInRect* as in *m_rcSquares[i].PtInRect (point)*, which returns a 1 if a mouse click is in square i.

A return of 1 means *return i* is executed (mouse click is in square i). A return of 0 means *return -1* is executed (click is not in square i).

Initialize data via *CTicTacToeDoc::OnNewDocument( )*. The data is stored in the array *m_nGameGrid[9]* where a 1 (one) represents an X (EX) and a 0 (zero) represents an O (OH). Initialize *m_nGameGrid[9]* by filing it with zeros.

**Code 809 Add code to existing OnNewDocument**

```
//BOOL CTicTacToeDoc::OnNewDocument()
//{
  if (!CDocument::OnNewDocument())   // do not copy
    return FALSE;   // do not copy
  // (SDI documents will reuse this document)
  ::ZeroMemory (m_nGameGrid, 9 * sizeof (int));
  m_nNextChar = EX;      // start with X

//   return TRUE;
//}
```

Data is initialized via *CTicTacToeDoc::OnNewDocument( )*.

MFC function *ZeroMemory* stores zeros in all elements of array *m_nGameGrid[9]*.

The game will start with the player who uses X, because variable *m_nNextChar = EX*.

As the game is played the X and O data is stored in the array *m_nGameGrid[9]* where a 1 (one) represents an X (EX) and a 0 (zero) represents an O (OH).

Programming with MFC

## 8.4 Code for View Functions

View code is placed in *TicTacToeView.h* and *TicTacToeView.cpp*

The view accesses document code via the *GetDocument* function by creating the pointer *pDoc*. Data read and write are enabled when the following code line is added to View functions.

*CTicTacToeDoc\* pDoc = GetDocument();*

> Use *pDoc* –> in View functions to read data from, and write data to, any document.

Examples: (note the addition of *View* to names fetching data)
1) READ – in what follows
*m_nNextChar* returns integer 0 or 1, which is assigned to
*m_nNextCharView*. In turn the integer is used in subsequent code lines.
   int m_nNextCharView = pDoc –> m_nNextChar;  // get data
   if (m_nNextCharView != EX)     // used here
   return;

2) READ – in what follows
*GetRectID* returns an integer, which is assigned to *GetRectIDView*. In turn the integer is assigned to *nPos*, which is used in subsequent code lines.

   int GetRectIDView = pDoc –> GetRectID (point);
   int nPos = GetRectIDView;

3) READ – in what follows
*nPos* is used in following code lines such as this one.

   int m_nGameGridView = pDoc –> m_nGameGrid[nPos] ;
   if ((nPos == –1) || (m_nGameGridView != 0))
   return;

4) WRITE – in what follows
Add an X to the game grid and set *m_nNextChar* to OH.
  pDoc –> m_nGameGrid[nPos] = EX;
  pDoc –> m_nNextChar = OH;

# 8 Tic Tac Toe - a Document/View Project

## 8.4.1 Code for Drawing on the Screen

The Tic Tac Toe board is defined by data array m_rcSquares[9].

We need to know where to draw an X or an O. This is why we need the number of the square a player clicked the mouse in. The data function *GetRectID* returns the number of that square (0 to 8). The function returns a –1 if the mouse was not clicked on a square. A data read fetches the number of the 'clicked' square.

The view functions *DrawX* and *DrawO* simply draw an X or an O.

The view function *DrawBoard* draws the 9 square grid and any X's or O's that players may have entered.

The data array *m_nGameGrid[i]* contains the players' X and O information.

> Add these two lines before the corresponding message handler lines in *TicTacToeView.cpp*.

///////////////////////////////////////////////////////////////
// CTicTacToeView support functions

**Code 810 Add Prototypes by hand under //*operations public* in *TicTacToeView.h*.**

```
void DrawX (CDC* pDC, int nPos);
void DrawO (CDC* pDC, int nPos);
void DrawBoard (CDC* pDC);
```

**Code 811 Add defines by hand after *#endif*, to the *TicTacToeView.cpp*.**

*#define EX 1*
*#define OH 2*

Programming with MFC

> Add functions by hand to *TicTacToeView.cpp* under support functions.

**Code 812 DrawX – add by hand**

```
void CTicTacToeView::DrawX (CDC* pDC, int nPos)
{
    CTicTacToeDoc* pDoc = GetDocument ();

    CRect m_rcSquaresView = pDoc -> m_rcSquares[nPos];   // get data

    CPen pen (PS_SOLID, 10, RGB (255, 0, 0));
    CPen* pOldPen = pDC -> SelectObject (&pen);

    CRect rect = m_rcSquaresView;
    rect.DeflateRect (16, 16);
    pDC -> MoveTo (rect.left, rect.top);
    pDC -> LineTo (rect.right, rect.bottom);
    pDC -> MoveTo (rect.left, rect.bottom);
    pDC -> LineTo (rect.right, rect.top);

    pDC -> SelectObject (pOldPen);
}
```

**nPos** The number of the square in which an X is to be drawn is stored in variable *nPos*.

**Arrow operator** pDC is a device context pointer [JP39]. A pointer accesses device context functions by using the arrow operator –>.

**Code 813 DrawO – add by hand**

```
void CTicTacToeView::DrawO (CDC* pDC, int nPos)
{
    CTicTacToeDoc* pDoc = GetDocument ();
        CRect m_rcSquaresView = pDoc -> m_rcSquares[nPos];   // get data
    CPen pen (PS_SOLID, 10, RGB (0, 0, 255));
    CPen* pOldPen = pDC -> SelectObject (&pen);
    pDC -> SelectStockObject (NULL_BRUSH);

    CRect rect = m_rcSquaresView;
    rect.DeflateRect (16, 16);
    pDC -> Ellipse (rect);
    pDC -> SelectObject (pOldPen);
}
```

# 8 Tic Tac Toe - a Document/View Project

**nPos**  The number of the square in which an O is to be drawn is stored in variable *nPos*.

SelectStockObject( ) is an MFC function [JP73].

The NULL_BRUSH parameter means the brush draws nothing [JP74] so that the background color is white in this case.

**Code 814 DrawBoard – add by hand**

```
void CTicTacToeView::DrawBoard (CDC* pDC)
{
    // Draw the lines that define the tic-tac-toe grid.
    CPen pen (PS_SOLID, 10, RGB (0, 0, 0));
    CPen* pOldPen = pDC ->SelectObject (&pen);
      pDC -> MoveTo (120, 16);
      pDC -> LineTo (120, 336);
    pDC -> MoveTo (232, 16);
    pDC -> LineTo (232, 336);
      pDC -> MoveTo (16, 120);
      pDC -> LineTo (336, 120);
    pDC -> MoveTo (16, 232);
    pDC -> LineTo (336, 232);

    // Draw the Xs and Os players have entered.
    CTicTacToeDoc* pDoc = GetDocument ();
    for (int i=0; i<9; i++) {
      int m_nGameGridView = pDoc -> m_nGameGrid[i];   // get data

      if (m_nGameGridView == EX)
        DrawX (pDC, i);
      else if (m_nGameGridView == OH)
        DrawO (pDC, i);
    }
    pDC ->SelectObject (pOldPen);
}
```

**Code 815 Add to *OnDraw* – add by hand**

```
  DrawBoard (pDC);
  pDC -> TextOut (400, 100, CString (_T ("For help click on HELP menu item")));
```

95

Programming with MFC

## 8.4.2 Code for Mouse Events and Message Handlers

Click on *View*, click on *ClassWizard*, click on *Message Maps*.
Important: Check project is *TicTacToe*, class name is *CTicTacToeView*.
In the *Object Ids* box click on *CTicTacToeView*
In the *Messages* box click on  *WM_LBUTTONDBLCLK*.
Click on *Add Function* to add *OnLButtonDblClk*.
Click on *Edit Code* to see function added as a skeleton message handler.

These actions add code items 1, 2, 3.

1) to *TicTacToeView.h* a prototype function in the message map
   *afx_msg void OnLButtonDblClk(UINT nFlags, CPoint point);*

2) to the message map in *TicTacToeView.cpp* the function
   *ON_WM_LBUTTONDBLCLK( )*.

3) in *TicTacToeView.cpp* a skeleton message handler
*void CTicTacToeView::OnLButtonDblClk(UINT nFlags, CPoint point)*

> Repeat for *WM_LBUTTONDOWN and WM_RBUTTONDOWN*.

**Code 816 Add *OnLButtonDblClk* code to *TicTacToeView.cpp* by hand**

```
void CTicTacToeView::OnLButtonDblClk(UINT nFlags, CPoint point)
{
    // TODO: Add your message handler code here and/or call default
    // Reset the game if one of the thick black lines defining the game
    // grid is double-clicked with the left mouse button.

    CTicTacToeDoc* pDoc = GetDocument ( );

    CDC* pDC = GetDC ( );
    if (pDC -> GetPixel (point) == RGB (0, 0, 0))     // reset if black pixel
    {   pDoc -> ResetGame ( );
        Invalidate ( );
    }
    ReleaseDC (pDC);
    CView::OnLButtonDblClk(nFlags, point);
}
```

Use F1 to fetch information about these functions used in *OnLButtonDblClk*.
CDC::GetPixel
COLORREF GetPixel( int *x*, int *y* ) const;
COLORREF GetPixel( POINT *point* ) const

*GetPixel* retrieves the RGB color value of the pixel at the point specified by *x* and *y*. The point must be in the clipping region. If the point is not in the clipping region the function has no effect and returns −1.

**Code 817 OnLButtonDown to *TicTacToeView.cpp* by hand**

```
void CTicTacToeView::OnLButtonDown(UINT nFlags, CPoint point)
{
  // TODO: Add your message handler code here and/or call default
  // Do nothing if it's O's turn, if the click occurred outside the
  // tic-tac-toe grid, or if a nonempty square was clicked.

  CTicTacToeDoc* pDoc = GetDocument ();

  int m_nNextCharView = pDoc -> m_nNextChar;   // get data
  if (m_nNextCharView != EX)
  return;

  int GetRectIDView = pDoc -> GetRectID (point);
  int nPos = GetRectIDView;
  int m_nGameGridView = pDoc -> m_nGameGrid[nPos];
  if ((nPos == -1) || (m_nGameGridView != 0))
  return;

  // Add an X to the game grid and toggle m_nNextChar.
  pDoc -> m_nGameGrid[nPos] = EX;
  pDoc -> m_nNextChar = OH;

  // Draw an X on the screen and see if either player has won.

  CDC* pDC = GetDC ();
  DrawX (pDC, nPos);
  ReleaseDC (pDC);

  pDoc -> CheckForGameOver ();

  CView::OnLButtonDown(nFlags, point);
}
```

Programming with MFC

**Code 818 OnRButtonDown to *TicTacToeView.cpp* by hand**

```
void CTicTacToeView::OnRButtonDown(UINT nFlags, CPoint point)
{
  // Do nothing if it's X's turn, if the click occurred outside the
  // tic-tac-toe grid, or if a nonempty square was clicked.

  CTicTacToeDoc* pDoc = GetDocument ();

  int m_nNextCharView = pDoc –> m_nNextChar;   // get data
  if (m_nNextCharView != OH)
  return;

  int GetRectIDView = pDoc –> GetRectID (point);
  int nPos = GetRectIDView;
  int m_nGameGridView = pDoc –> m_nGameGrid[nPos];
  if ((nPos == -1) || (m_nGameGridView != 0))
  return;

  // Add an O to the game grid and toggle m_nNextChar.
  pDoc –> m_nGameGrid[nPos] = OH;
  pDoc –> m_nNextChar = EX;

  // Draw an O on the screen and see if either player has won.
  CDC* pDC = GetDC ();
  DrawO (pDC, nPos);
  ReleaseDC (pDC);

  pDoc -> CheckForGameOver ();

  CView::OnRButtonDown(nFlags, point);
}
```

## 8.5 Code for Menu Items

The menus listed across the top of the TicTacToe window are in the *top-level* menu. Clicking on a menu produces a *drop-down* menu consisting of a list of one or more *menu items*. The intent here is to add a *HELP* menu item, and a *Reset* menu item (as an alternative to left button double clicking),

**1)** Click *ResourceView* pane. Click on +TicTacToe resources. Click on +*Menu*, double click on *IDR_MAINFRAME*.

# 8 Tic Tac Toe - a Document/View Project

**2)** In the menu bar, right click on *File* menu item *New*. Right click on *Properties*.
   change *ID_FILE_NEW* to *ID_FILE_RESET*
   change the caption to *&Reset\tCtrl+R*
   click on X.

**3)** Create a message handler for the *Reset* menu item.

In Fileview click on *CTicTacToeView.cpp*
In the *View* menu click on *ClassWizard* to open *MFC ClassWizard*.
   Important: Set Project to *TicTacToe*, classname to **CTicTacToeView**.
   In Object IDs click on *ID_FILE_RESET*.
   In Messages click on *COMMAND*.
   Click on *Add Function* button.
   *OnFileReset* appears in the Add Member Functions name box.
   Click on OK.
   Click on Edit code button to get *CTicTacToeView::OnFileReset*.

Verify *ON_COMMAND(ID_FILE_RESET, OnFileReset)* is in the *TicTacToeView.cpp* message map.

Verify that *afx_msg void OnFileReset(); is in TicTacToeView.h*.
Add Code 819 to *TicTacToeView.cpp*.

**Code 819 OnFileReset to *TicTacToeView.cpp* by hand**

```
void CTicTacToeView::OnFileReset()
{
  CTicTacToeDoc* pDoc = GetDocument ();
  CDC* pDC = GetDC ();
  {
    pDoc -> ResetGame ();
    Invalidate ( );
  }
  ReleaseDC (pDC);
}
```

**4)** In the *ResourceView IDR_MAINFRAME* menu bar, click on *Help* to see the drop down menu items. Click on the blank menu item. Right click on *Properties*.
   change the blank ID to *ID_HELP1* (to avoid conflict with Visual help)
   change the caption to *&Help*
   click on X

Programming with MFC

5) Create a message handler for the *HELP* menu item.

In Fileview click on *CTicTacToeView.cpp*
In the C++ *View* menu click on *ClassWizard* to open *MFC ClassWizard*.
  Important: Set Project to *TicTacToe*, classname to *CTicTacToeView*.
  In Object IDs click on *ID_HELP1*.
  In Messages click on *COMMAND*.
  Click on *Add Function* button.
  *OnHelp1* appears in the Add Member Functions box.
  Click on OK.
  Click on Edit code button to get *TicTacToeView::OnHelp1*

Verify that *ON_COMMAND(ID_HELP, OnHelp1)* is in the *TicTacToeView.cpp* message map.

Verify that *afx_msg void OnHelp1();* is in *TicTacToeView.h*.

Add Code 820 to *TicTacToeView.cpp*.

**Code 820 Add OnHelp1 to *TicTacToeView.cpp* by hand**

```
void CMainFrame::OnHelp1( )
{
   // TODO: Add your command handler code here
   CString strHELP;

   strHELP = (CString)
   "Left button click on a square to enter an X."
   + "\n"
   + "Right button click on a square to enter an O."
   + "\n"
   + "Left button double click on a grid line to clear the board and start a new game."
   + "\n"
   + "Click menu item RESET to clear the board and start a new game."
   + "\n"
   ;
    AfxMessageBox (strHELP, MB_ICONEXCLAMATION | MB_OK, 0);
}
```

# 9 ADD

This *project* produces the ADD program that takes a user through the series of steps required to execute the task, which is the addition of two integers according to the *Standard Addition Algorithm with Carry* (see the sidebar on page 102).

How do you create a program? Well, in this case a theory is available that provides a basis for the program design. A theory cast in the form of an algorithm, which is most convenient. The example on the next page shows the sequence of steps that add two 5-digit numbers. The algorithm assumes you know how to add one-digit numbers ranging from 0 to 9.

If a user does not know how to add one-digit numbers *ADD* can present two one-digit numbers so that the user can practice doing just that. By practice we mean the user can enter a digit he thinks is the correct answer, *ADD* says the answer is correct or wrong, and if wrong *ADD* shows the correct answer. By this very simple trail and error method a user can learn how to add two one-digit numbers. The point is the algorithm's limitation is overcome and a teacher is not required.

As for the largest numbers available to be added we *arbitrarily* select 5 digit numbers whose range is 00000 to 99999. Furthermore a user should be able to add two numbers with different numbers of digits. Therefore the program needs to ask the user to enter the two numbers to be added that satisfy his desires. That is one version of the program.

Another version focuses on the number of digits in the two numbers. Consequently the program asks for the numbers of digits, while generating the corresponding numbers by using a random number generator.

In what follows we implement the version where the user selects the numbers of digits, and the program produces the numbers to be added.

Programming with MFC

***Standard Addition Algorithm with Carry*** (Add 56913 to 60388)

**Step 1**: Execute a one digit addition-with-carry in position 0.

Add the units $8+3 = 11 = 1 \times 10 + 1$
Enter the unit's 1 in answer position 0, and the ten's 1 in carry position 1.

```
      1
  60388
+ 56913
───────
      1
```

**Step 2**: Execute a one digit addition-with-carry in position 1.

Add the tens $1+8+1 = 10 = 1 \times 10 + 0$
Enter the unit's 0 in answer position 1, and the ten's 1 in carry position 2.

```
     11
  60388
+ 56913
───────
     01
```

**Step 3**: Execute a one digit addition-with-carry in position 2.

Add the hundreds $1+3+9 = 13 = 1 \times 10 + 3$
Enter the unit's 3 in answer position 2, and the ten's 1 in carry position 3.

```
    111
  60388
+ 56913
───────
    301
```

**Step 4**: Execute a one digit addition-with-carry in position 3.

Add the thousands $1+0+6 = 07 = 0 \times 10 + 7$
Enter the unit's 7 in answer position 3, and the ten's 0 in carry position 4.

```
   0111
  60388
+ 56913
───────
   7301
```

**Step 5**: Execute a one digit addition-with-carry in position 4.

Add the ten thousands $0+6+5 = 11 = 1 \times 10 + 1$
Enter the unit's 1 in answer position 4, and the ten's 1 in carry position 5.

```
  10111
  60388
+ 56913
───────
  17301
```

**Step 6**: Execute a one digit addition-with-carry in position 5.

Add the hundred thousands $1+0+0 = 01 = 0 \times 10 + 1$
Enter the unit's 1 in answer position 5, and the ten's 0 in carry position 6 (not shown). Since the carry is 0 we are done.

```
  10111
  60388
+ 56913
───────
 117301
```

# 9 ADD

**Events drive the program** The *windows program execution process* is very different from a conventional program that executes instructions sequentially [JP4, 12].

Windows programs are driven by *events*. In the *ADD* program events are a user clicking a mouse button, a user pressing a key, or an executing function creating events that issue messages.

The *ADD* program responds to each event by issuing a windows message, which is placed in the window's message queue. A message exits the queue when it calls the corresponding *ADD* program's message handler *OnChar*. In this way the program executes as events are translated into actions.

In this version of *ADD* the focus is on the number of digits in the two numbers. Consequently the program asks for two numbers of digits, and then generates the numbers by using a random number generator.

There are two program phases: *setup the problem* and *do the problem*.

The program starts with *OnDraw* painting the screen [JP504], which in effect requests a key press processed by *OnChar* [JP153] followed by a call to *Invalidate* (that repaints the screen) to complete a cycle of events- *OnDraw, OnChar, Invalidate*. A cycle of events executes the first part *setting up the problem* or the second part *doing the problem*.

The cycle of events changes to *doing the problem* when a *setting up the problem* yes response to the y, n request for a key press starts the *do the problem* mode, which is drawn on the screen by *OnDraw* (Figure 901 page 105). A no response starts over.

The user is asked to select the number of digits in the first number. The user responds by typing a 5 for example. This key press is processed by *OnChar*.[JP151], which stores the ASCII character 5 in a buffer, converts the 5 to an integer saved in a variable, and calls the function *Invalidate* that orders *OnDraw* to redraw the screen showing the 5 in the caret position (Figure 901).

The process repeats when the user is asked to select the number of digits in the second number (the 4 in Figure 901).

Programming with MFC

The process repeats once more when the user is asked for a yes or no response to a request to do the problem.

By design *switch* functions in *OnChar* define the active keys as
    Enter, Backspace, q, Q, y, Y, n, N, and 0 to 9.
All other keys simply pass through the switch functions doing nothing.

The major players:
  virtual void OnDraw(CDC* pDC);
  afx_msg void OnChar(UINT nChar, UINT nRepCnt, UINT nFlags);

The setup and do selection variables:
  int m_nStart, m_nDigit, m_ni;

A font function that allows selection of font size:
  void SelectAFont(int n,CDC* pDC);
  CFont* m_pOldFont;

The random number generator:
  void seed();
  long RandRange(long min, long max);
  void Numbers(int nd1, int nd2);

The caret controls:
  afx_msg void OnKillFocus(CWnd* pNewWnd);
  afx_msg void OnSetFocus(CWnd* pOldWnd);

The help program selection button:
  afx_msg void OnRButtonDown(UINT nFlags, CPoint point);

---

Create the ADD workspace and build the ADD skeleton project per Chapter 1 Sections 1.1, 1.4, 1.5.

---

Code is added only to *AddView.h*, *AddView.cpp*, and resource files. There are no data files in this document/view workspace.

9 ADD

**Figure 901 Set up the Problem**

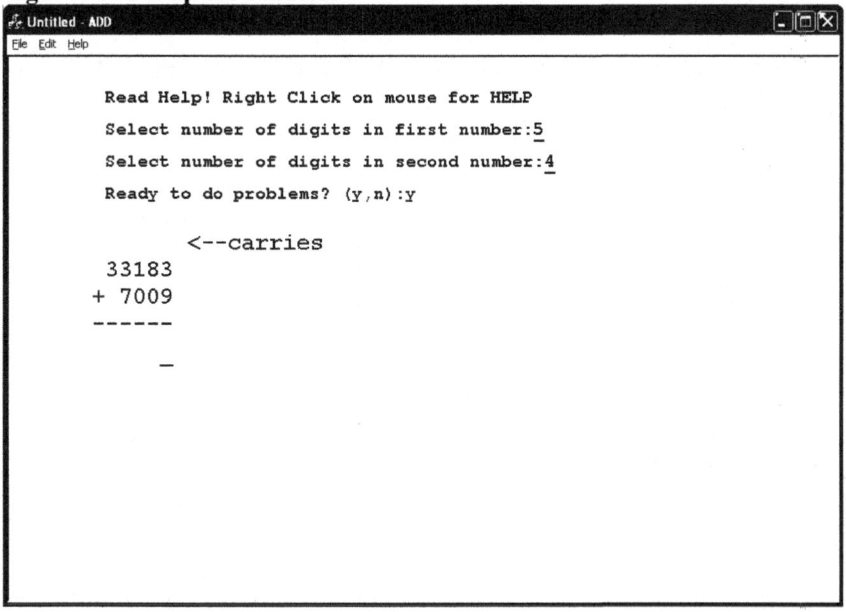

```
Read Help! Right Click on mouse for HELP
Select number of digits in first number:5
Select number of digits in second number:4
Ready to do problems? (y,n):y

         <--carries
   33183
 +  7009
   ------
       _
```

**Figure 902 Do the Problem**

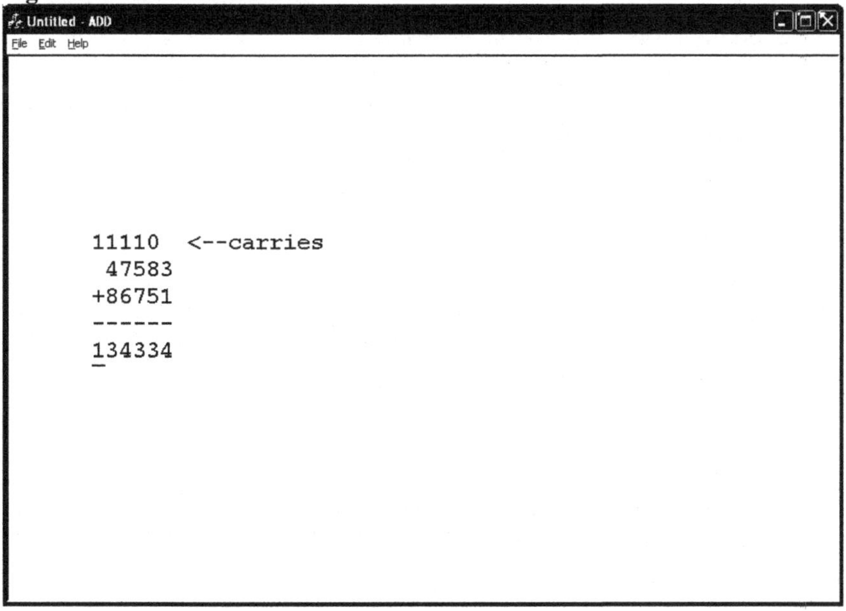

```
   11110   <--carries
    47583
   +86751
   ------
   134334
   _
```

Programming with MFC

**Events move the ADD program along.**

*Keyboard key presses and mouse button clicks generate the action messages for the arithmetic program steps. The action messages change the values of variables so that the program moves on to the next step.*

Part 1: set up the problem (variable *m_nstart* = 0)

1 "Select number of digits ($d_1$ = 1 to 5) in first number:"
    User responds by entering digit $d_1$ and pressing enter.

2 "Select number of digits ($d_2$ = 1 to 5) in second number:"
    User responds by entering digit $d_2$ and pressing enter.

3 "Ready to do problems (yes, no)?"
    User responds by entering y or n and pressing enter. A yes moves the program on *to do* the problem. A no returns to step 1.

A random number generator produces numbers $n_1$ and $n_2$ with number of digits $d_1$ and $d_2$, which are painted on the screen.

Part 2: do the problem (variable *m_nstart* = 1)

A *caret* that moves along marks slots where the user is supposed to enter digits as the solution process progresses.

Fill in the slots (do the problem). After each problem slot is filled with a digit, or passed over, the control variable *m_ni* is set to 1.

Then, depending on the user's "solution" to the problem, one of the following messages is displayed in a message dialog box. The messages require a yes or no answer.
Case 1
    IF statement "*Correct! Do a new problem?*"
        Yes sets up a new problem with new d1 and d2.
    ELSE statement "*Not correct. TRY IT AGAIN?*"
        Yes sets up the same problem with same d1 and d2.
Case 2: *DO A NEW PROBLEM?*
    Yes sets up a new problem with same d1 and d2.
Case 3: *Quit (on No you start over)*
    Yes quits the program.
    No returns to part 1 so that user can start over.

# 9 ADD

## 9.1 Preparing *OnDraw* and *OnChar*

The major players in the *ADD* program are the functions *OnDraw* and *OnChar*. The *ADD* workspace in Visual C++ automatically includes *OnDraw*. *OnChar* is not included.

**Add OnChar for Message Passing**
Click on View, click on Class Wizard, click on Message Maps.

**Figure 903 Shows that WM_CHAR message has been added**

Important: Verify Project is *ADD*, Class is **CADDView** (Figure 903).
In the *Object IDs* box click on *CADDView*.
In the *Messages* box click on *WM_CHAR*..
This activates the *Add Function* button.
Click on *Add Function* to add *OnChar* to *ADDView.cpp*.
Click on edit code to see the *OnChar* function.
Click on OK. This adds code items 1, 2, 3.

1) to *ADDView.h* a prototype function
   *afx_msg void OnChar(UINT nChar, UINT nRepCnt, UINT nFlags);*
2) to the message map in *ADDView.cpp* the function
   ON_WM_CHAR()
3) in *ADDView.cpp* a skeleton message handler.
*void CADDView::OnChar(UINT nChar, UINT nRepCnt, UINT nFlags)*

107

Programming with MFC

The design divides into two parts: *setup the problem (m_nStart = 0)* and *do the problem (m_nStart = 1)*. The design starts by using the function *OnDraw* to draw on the screen the *setup the problem* questions the user is asked to answer (Figure 901). A yes answer switches to the *do the problem* mode producing two random numbers, with the selected number of digits, and drawing the problem on the screen (Figures 901, 902). The user then does the problem by entering digits in slots.

**OnDraw** The *OnDraw* function (in *ADDview.cpp*) draws on the screen the current status of the problem the user is solving. E.g. partial digit sums and carries are drawn immediately after a digit entry by the user. *OnDraw* does not change the value of any variables. The functions in *OnChar* respond to key presses to enter (solution) digits and change variable values. The responses to any key differ according to the modes *Setup* or *Do*. The *OnDraw* and *OnChar* set up and do structures have two parts, marked as Setup and Do, which are activated according to the value of variable *m_nStart* (Code 901). The skeletons are filled in as we proceed.

All key presses are processed by message handlers in *OnChar*. *Invalidate* calls *OnDraw* to repaint the screen

**Code 901 *OnDraw* Setup and Do structure – add code** by hand

```
int m_nStart;      // add to ADDView.h Implementation public

void CAddView::OnDraw(CDC* pDC)   // add to ADDView.cpp
{
  if (m_nStart==0)    //  Setup
  {  } // setup the problem
  if (m_nStart==1)          //  Do
  {  } // display and do the problem
}    //end of OnDraw
```

**Code 902 OnChar Set up and Do – add code by hand to *ADDView.cpp***

```
void CAddView::OnChar(UINT nChar, UINT nRepCnt, UINT nFlags)
{
  if (m_nStart==0)   // Setup
  {  } // key press responses setup the problem
  if (m_nStart==1)   // Do
  {  } // key press responses display and do the problem
}    //end of OnChar
```

# 9 ADD

## 9.2 The Caret and the Font

**Caret** The *caret* is the flashing horizontal (or vertical) bar used by applications to mark the point (aka slot) on the screen where the next text character will be inserted when a key is pressed [JP154].

A key press creates a keyboard message. Keyboard messages are sent to the window that has the "input focus" [JP144]. The "focus" message names are WM_SETFOCUS and WM_KILLFOCUS. The associated functions are *OnSetFocus* and *OnKillfocus*. These two functions are used to create and destroy the caret as focus is gained and lost by a window. Class Wizard facilitates adding these two functions.

Click on View, click on Class Wizard, click on Message Maps.

**Figure 904 Shows that WM_KILLFOCUS message has been added**

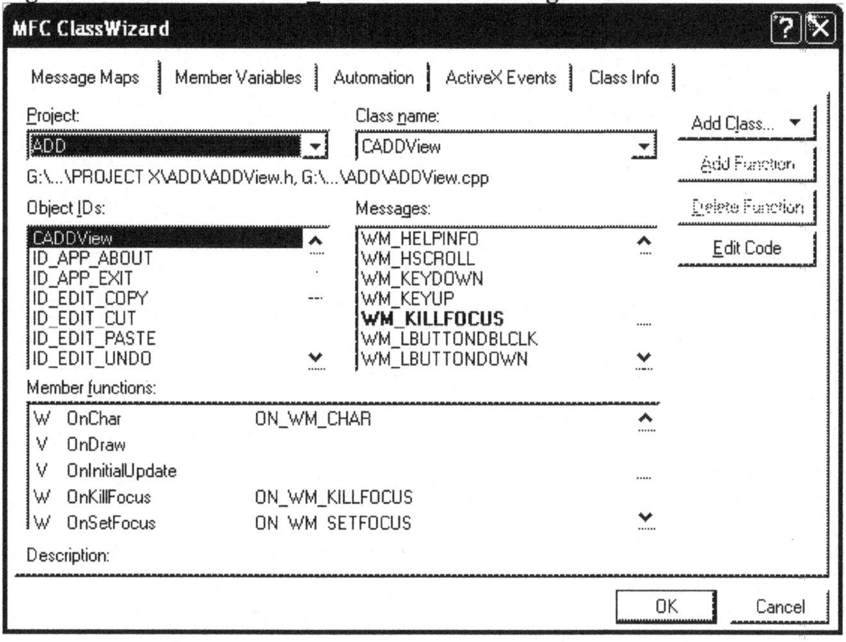

Important: Verify Project is *ADD*, Class is *CADDView* (Figure 904).
In the *Object IDs* box click on *CADDView*.
In the *Messages* box click *WM_KILLFOCUS*.
This activates the *Add Function* button.
Click on *Add Function* to add *OnKillFocus* to *ADDView.cpp*.
Click on edit code to see the *OnKillFocus* function.

109

Programming with MFC

Click on OK. This adds code items 1, 2, 3.
1) to *ADDView.h* a prototype function
   *afx_msg void OnKillFocus(CWnd* pNewWnd);*
2) to the message map in *ADDView.cpp* the function
   *ON_WM_KILLFOCUS()*
3) in *ADDView.cpp* a skeleton message handler.
void CADDView::OnKillFocus(CWnd* pNewWnd)

> Repeat this process to add *OnSetFocus*.

**Code 903 add to private in *ADDView.h* by hand**

```
CPoint m_ptCaretPos;     // Implementation public:
int  m_nxChar, m_nyChar;   // also used by font function
```

**Code 904 add to *ADDView.cpp* by hand**

```
void CADDView::OnKillFocus(CWnd* pNewWnd)
{
  CView::OnKillFocus(pNewWnd);
  // TODO: Add your message handler code here
  HideCaret();
  m_ptCaretPos = GetCaretPos();
  ::DestroyCaret();
}
```

**Code 905 add to *ADDView.cpp* by hand**

```
void CADDView::OnSetFocus(CWnd* pOldWnd)
{
  CView::OnSetFocus(pOldWnd);
  // TODO: Add your message handler code here
  CreateSolidCaret(m_nxChar,max(2,::GetSystemMetrics(SM_CYBORDER)));
  SetCaretPos(m_ptCaretPos);
  ShowCaret();
}
```

# 9 ADD

**Font** We desire different font point heights for setup the problem and do the problem. The program uses two font sizes; one for requesting user input to setup the problem (TEXTF) and another for the problem (PROBF).

**Code 906 Font defines. Add to *ADDView.cpp. by hand***

```
#define TEXTF 14    //nlp text font size
#define PROBF 18    //nlp problem font size
```

This is why we created a "Courier New" font with font point height $n$ as a parameter [JP69]. *SelectAFont(n, pDC)*, as written (Code 908), creates a "Courier New" font with size n points. When font size is changed caret size is also changed. Add *SelectAFont* to ADDView.cpp.

**Code 907 *SelectAFont* prototype and a variable. Add to *ADDView.h by hand***

```
public:
  void SelectAFont(int n,CDC* pDC);
  CFont* m_pOldFont;
```

**Code 908 Font Function Add to *ADDView.cpp by hand***

```
void CADDView::SelectAFont(int n, CDC *pDC)
{
  int nHeight = - ((pDC -> GetDeviceCaps(LOGPIXELSY) * n) / 72);

  CFont aFont;                         //create font object
  aFont.CreateFont(nHeight, 0, 0, 0,
        FW_BOLD, FALSE, FALSE, 0, DEFAULT_CHARSET,
        OUT_TT_PRECIS, CLIP_DEFAULT_PRECIS,
        DEFAULT_QUALITY, FIXED_PITCH | FF_MODERN,
        "Courier New");

  m_pOldFont = pDC -> SelectObject(&aFont);

  //get char dimensions
  TEXTMETRIC tm;
  pDC -> GetTextMetrics(&tm);
  m_nxChar = tm.tmAveCharWidth;
  m_nyChar = tm.tmHeight + tm.tmExternalLeading;
}
```

Programming with MFC

## 9.3 Setting Up the Problem

Setting up the problem requires selection of two numbers of digits for the random numbers to be added, and a yes/no decision. In order to do this the user is asked two questions selecting the numbers of digits, and asked one question to make a yes/no decision. The questions take the form of text drawn on the screen [JP67] (Figure 901). This requires drawing strings, the caret, and ultimately the key press responses in defined positions.

MFC provides the necessary functions:
*MoveTo*       changes the current position to the given x,y coordinates.
*SetTextAlign* updates the current position for text (TA_UPDATECP).
*TextOut*      prints the text that is inside the quotes.

For example;
  pDC −> MoveTo(x1,y1+2*(TEXTF+2));
  pDC −> SetTextAlign(TA_UPDATECP);
  pDC −> TextOut(0,0,"Select number of digits in first number: ");

  pDC −> SetTextAlign(TA_UPDATECP | TA_RIGHT);
  pDC −> TextOut(0,0,m_nChar1);  // paints the selected number of digits

Many variables are required to store the current state of the program. Here are the variables required to setup and display the problem.

| Variable | Purpose |
| --- | --- |
| int m_nDigit | selects the question to be asked |
| CPoint m_ptCaretPos | current caret position |
| int m_nxChar, m_nyChar | caret position coordinates |
|  |  |
| UINT m_nChar1, m_nChar2, | numbers of digits |
| UNIT m_nCharYN | y/n answer |
| UNIT m_nChar | character pressed by any key |
|  |  |
|  |  |

MFC provides the *OnInitialUpdate* function that allows for initializing variables when the program starts.

112

# 9 ADD

> Add the *OnInitialUpdate* support function.

Click on View, click on Class Wizard, click on Message Maps.
Important: Verify Project is *ADD*, Class is *CADDView* (Figure 904).
In the *Object IDs* box click on *CADDView*.
In the *Messages* box click *OnInitialUpdate*.
This activates the *Add Function* button.
Click on *Add Function* to add *OnInitialUpdate* to *ADDView.cpp*.
Click on edit code to see the *OnInitialUpdate* function.
Click on OK.
This process adds the usual code items 1 and 3 (no 2).
1) *virtual void OnInitialUpdate();* in *ADDView.h*
3) *void CADDView::OnInitialUpdate()* in *ADDView.cpp*

### Code 909 Variables - Add Code to *ADDview.h*.

```
private:
   UINT m_nChar1, m_nChar2, m_nChar, m_nCharYN;
public:
   int m_nDigit;
```

### Code 910 Initialized variables - Add to OnInitialUpdate() in *ADDview.cpp*.

```
m_nStart = 0;
m_nDigit = 1;
m_nChar1 = ' ';
m_nChar2 = ' ';
m_nChar = ' ';
m_nCharYN = ' ';
```

The functions *MoveTo*, *SetTextAlign*, and *TextOut* are used repeatedly to query the user. And the following are used to update the caret position.
   m_ptCaretPos = pDC -> GetCurrentPosition();
   m_ptCaretPos.y += m_nyChar;
   SetCaretPos(m_ptCaretPos);

Use /*     */ to comment out the function void CADDView::OnDraw(CDC* pDC)
Replace it with code 911 on the next page.

Programming with MFC

### Code 911 Setup the problem - Add *OnDraw* in *ADDview.cpp*.

```cpp
void CADDView::OnDraw(CDC* pDC)
{
  CADDDoc* pDoc = GetDocument();
  ASSERT_VALID(pDoc);
  // TODO: add draw code for native data here
  int x0=100,y0=200,x1=100,y1=30;

  if (m_nStart==0)        //  A1
  {
    SelectAFont(TEXTF,pDC);
    CreateSolidCaret(m_nxChar,max(2,::GetSystemMetrics(SM_CYBORDER)));

    // setup the problem
    if (m_nDigit >= 1)
    {
      //  user selects 1,2,3,4, or 5 and presses Enter
      pDC -> MoveTo(x1,y1);
      pDC -> SetTextAlign(TA_UPDATECP);
      pDC -> TextOut(0,0,"Read Help! Right Click on mouse for HELP");

      pDC -> MoveTo(x1,y1+2*(TEXTF+2));
      pDC -> SetTextAlign(TA_UPDATECP);
      pDC -> TextOut(0,0,"Select number of digits in first number: ");

      pDC -> SetTextAlign(TA_UPDATECP | TA_RIGHT);
      pDC -> TextOut(0,0,m_nChar1);

      m_ptCaretPos = pDC -> GetCurrentPosition();
      m_ptCaretPos.y += m_nyChar;
      SetCaretPos(m_ptCaretPos);
    }

    if (m_nDigit >= 2)
    {
      // user selects 1,2,3,4, or 5 and presses Enter
          pDC -> MoveTo(x1, y1+4*(TEXTF+2));
      pDC -> SetTextAlign(TA_UPDATECP);
      pDC -> TextOut(0,0,"Select number of digits in second number: ");

      pDC -> SetTextAlign(TA_UPDATECP | TA_RIGHT);
      pDC -> TextOut(0,0,m_nChar2);

      m_ptCaretPos = pDC -> GetCurrentPosition();
      m_ptCaretPos.y += m_nyChar;
      SetCaretPos(m_ptCaretPos);
    }

    if (m_nDigit == 3)
    {
      // print y or n selected by user     y sets m_nStart = 1
```

# 9 ADD

```
        pDC->MoveTo(x1,y1+6*(TEXTF+2));
        pDC->SetTextAlign(TA_UPDATECP);
        pDC->TextOut(0,0,"Ready to do problems? (y,n): ");

        pDC->SetTextAlign(TA_UPDATECP | TA_RIGHT);
        pDC->TextOut(0,0,m_nCharYN);

        m_ptCaretPos = pDC -> GetCurrentPosition();
        m_ptCaretPos.y += m_nyChar;
        SetCaretPos(m_ptCaretPos);
    }
  } //end of m_nStart==0 setup

// add code 913 here
} //end of OnDraw
```

---

UINT SetTextAlign( UINT *nFlags* );
*nFlags* specifies text-alignment flags. The flags specify the relationship between a point and a rectangle that bounds the text. Here are two flags.

TA_RIGHT Aligns the point with the right side of a bounding rectangle.
TA_UPDATECP Updates the current x-position after each call to a text-output function. The new position is at the right side of the bounding rectangle for the text. When this flag is set, the coordinates specified in calls to the **TextOut** member function are ignored, which is why the 0, 0.

TextOut writes the string to the screen starting at the updated specified location (the x, y coordinates) using the currently selected font.

Writing the string moved the current text position to the end of the string. *SetTextAlign* updates the current position for text. It aligns this new current position with the right side of the text box. (TA_UPDATECP | TA_RIGHT). The TextOut String writes a character in the text box. Initially m_nChar1 stores a space so you only see the caret. When a key is pressed the key character is placed over the blinking caret.

If user presses active key w, then char w replaces the space in m_nChar1 and the screen is redrawn with char w over the caret.

Note: until Enter is pressed user can press any active key which replaces w. The user can press any set of active keys any number of times.
The caret is repositioned whenever an x,y move occurs.

Programming with MFC

## 9.4 Displaying the Problem

Displaying the problem requires painting text lines (Figure 901). The TextOut function CString parameter can be a character array (Code 912), which we determined by trying that. (MFC F1 key explanations are incomplete sometimes.)

BOOL TextOut( int *x*, int *y*, const CString& *str* );
Return Value Nonzero if the function is successful; otherwise 0.
Parameters:
*x* Specifies the logical x-coordinate of the starting point of the text.
*y* Specifies the logical y-coordinate of the starting point of the text.
*str* A CString object that contains the characters to be drawn.

**Remarks**
Writes a character string at the specified location using the currently selected font. Character origins are at the upper-left corner of the character cell. By default, the current position is not used or updated by the function.
If an application needs to update the current position when it calls **TextOut**, the application can call the **SetTextAlign** member function with *nFlags* set to **TA_UPDATECP**. When this flag is set, Windows ignores the *x* and *y* parameters on subsequent calls to **TextOut**, using the current position instead.

**Code 912 Display the problem variables - Add to *ADDview.h* by hand**

```
#define WIDTH 8
long m_lresult;
int m_nd1, m_nd2;

char m_szResult[WIDTH];
char m_szCarry[WIDTH];
char m_szLine[WIDTH];
char m_szN1[WIDTH];
char m_szN2[WIDTH];
```

# 9 ADD

## Code 913 Display the problem - Add *OnDraw* in *ADDview.cpp* by hand

```
if (m_nStart==1) //     display the problem
{
  SelectAFont(PROBF,pDC);
  CreateSolidCaret(m_nxChar,max(2,::GetSystemMetrics(SM_CYBORDER)));

  if (m_lresult>9)
  {
    pDC->TextOut(x0+(m_nd1+1)*m_nxChar,y0-m_nyChar,"<--carries");

    pDC->MoveTo(x0+(m_nd1 - 1)*m_nxChar,y0-m_nyChar);
    pDC->SetTextAlign(TA_UPDATECP | TA_RIGHT);
    pDC->TextOut(0,0,m_szCarry);
  }

  pDC->MoveTo(x0+(m_nd1)*m_nxChar,y0);
  pDC->SetTextAlign(TA_UPDATECP | TA_RIGHT);
  pDC->TextOut(0,0,m_szN1);

  pDC->MoveTo(x0+(m_nd1)*m_nxChar,y0+m_nyChar);
  pDC->SetTextAlign(TA_UPDATECP | TA_RIGHT);
  pDC->TextOut(0,0,m_szN2);

  pDC->MoveTo(x0-m_nxChar,y0+m_nyChar);
  pDC->SetTextAlign(TA_UPDATECP);
  pDC->TextOut(0,0,"+");

  pDC->MoveTo(x0-m_nxChar,y0+2*m_nyChar);
  pDC->SetTextAlign(TA_UPDATECP);
  pDC->TextOut(0,0,m_szLine);

  pDC->MoveTo(x0+(m_nd1)*m_nxChar,y0+3*m_nyChar);
  pDC->SetTextAlign(TA_UPDATECP | TA_RIGHT);
  pDC->TextOut(0,0,m_szResult);
}
// add code 922 here
```

Programming with MFC

## 9.5 Creating the Numbers to Add

Here is how the two integers to be added are created. User is asked to select number-of-digits $d_1$ and $d_2$ that are *converted to integers m_nd1* and *m_nd2* in Code 921 cases 1, 2, 3, 4, 5 on page 124. Selections greater than 5 are rejected.

If $d_1 < d_2$ then $d_1$ and $d_2$ are exchanged so that $d_1 > d_2$.

The function *Numbers* generates the long integers $m\_ln_1$ and $m\_ln_2$ with numbers of digits corresponding to $d_1$ and $d_2$. Here is how *Numbers* does that.

*Numbers* uses *integers m_nd1* and *m_nd2* to calculate maximum long integers $m\_lmx1 = 10^{\wedge}m\_nd1$ and $m\_lmx2 = 10^{\wedge}m\_nd2$. Then the max numbers are used by *RandRange* to produce two random long integers $m\_ln_1$ and $m\_ln_2$, which will be added. For example $d_1 = 3$ then $m\_lmx1 = 1000$ and $m\_ln_1$ is randomly select from the range $100 <= m\_ln_1 < 1000$ so that $m\_ln_1$ is in the range 100 to 999. The correct answer $m\_lresult = m\_ln1 + m\_ln2$ is saved.

The user's answer to the problem *m_lanswer* is compared to *m_lresult* so that the users' answer can be marked correct or not correct.

The digit sums and carries are placed in *slots* as the addition is implemented. The number of slots in the problem, *maxslot*, is calculated. For example, if $d_1$ is 3 then $maxslot = 2*m\_nd1 + 1 - 2*tx = 2*3 + 1 - 2*tx$.

**Code 914 Add prototypes and variables to *ADDView.h* by hand**

```
void seed();              //nlp all public
long RandRange(long min, long max);
void Numbers(int nd1, int nd2);

long m_lmx1, m_lmx2;   // 10^m_nd1, 10^m_nd2
long m_ln1, m_ln2;     // numbers to add
int m_nmaxslot;        // number of slots to fill as an answer
```

**Code 915 Add define and include to *ADDView.cpp* hand**

```
#include <cmath>      //nlp
#define RANGE(i, mn, mx) (i>=mn) && (i<mx) ? 0:1
```

118

# 9 ADD

**Code 916 Add Rand Range to *ADDView.cpp* by hand**

```
long CADDView::RandRange(long min, long max)
{
  long int r;
  do {
    if (min >=10000) {r = 9 * rand();}
    else {r = rand();}
  }while (RANGE(r,min,max));
  return r;
}
```

**Code 917 Add Seed to *ADDView.cpp* by hand**

```
void CADDView::seed()
{
  int utime;
  long ltime;
  ltime = time(NULL);          // requires time.h
  utime = (unsigned int) ltime/2;
  srand(utime);                // requires stdlib.h
}
```

**Code 918 Add Numbers to *ADDView.cpp* by hand**

```
void CADDView::Numbers(int nd1,int nd2)
{
  m_lmx1 = (long) pow((double)10,(double)nd1);   //mx1 = 10^m_nd1
  m_lmx2 = (long) pow((double)10,(double)nd2);   //mx2 = 10^m_nd2

  m_ln1 = RandRange(m_lmx1/10,m_lmx1);
  m_ln2 = RandRange(m_lmx2/10,m_lmx2);
  //random selection of n1 & n2

  m_lresult = m_ln1 + m_ln2;  //will need to compare to user's answer

  int tx;     // e.g. if sum of two 3-digt numbers is xxx (tx=1) or yyyy (tx=0)
  if (m_lresult < m_lmx1) tx = 1; else tx = 0;
  m_nmaxslot = 2*nd1 + 1 - 2*tx;
}
```

## 9.6 A Key Press Skeleton

**Code 919** <u>Do not install this code</u> **User Setup and Do The Problem Key Presses are Processed by switch functions such as these.**

```
void CAddView::OnChar(UINT nChar, UINT nRepCnt, UINT nFlags)
{
    if(m_nStart==0)    // Setup
    {
      switch(nChar)
      {
        case VK_RETURN:   //Enter key
        case VK_BACK:     //Backspace key
        case 'Y':
        case 'y':
        case 'N':
        case 'n':
        case 'Q':
        case 'q':
        case '1':
        case '2':
        case '3':
        case '4':
        case '5':
        default:         // any other key - do nothing
      } //end of switch
      Invalidate(FALSE);   // redraw the screen
    } //end of m_nstart==0 if
    else    //start of m_nstart==1    // Do
    {
      switch(nChar)
      {
        case VK_RETURN:   //Enter key 1
        case VK_BACK:     //Backspace key 0
        case 'Y':   //0
        case 'y':
        case 'N':   //0
        case 'n':
        case 'Q':
        case 'q': //quit 0
        case '1':   //0
          through
        case '9':   //0
        default:     // any other key do nothing
      } //end of switch
      Invalidate(FALSE);   // redraw the screen
    } //end of m_nstart==1 else
}
```

## 9.7 Processing Setup-the-Problem Key Presses

Every key press generates a *WM_CHAR* message that calls the *OnChar* function, which includes two *switch* functions: one for problem setup and one for doing the problem. The *cases* in the *switch* functions define active keys. (Code 914 page 120)

The *WM_CHAR* messages created by inactive keys are discarded by the switch functions. Here are the key presses that set up the problem:

**1, 2, 3, 4, 5** The user presses a key in the range 1 to 5 as a response to
"Select number of digits in first number:"
"Select number of digits in second number."

User can type over digits (1 to 5) to change entries. Nevertheless, if the user presses any sequence of keys (except Enter) only the numbers 1 to 5 will be painted. Pressing Enter moves to the next request.

**Y, y** User presses the Y key to move on to do the problem.
**N, n** User presses the N key to start over.

**Backspace** Before enter is pressed the user can backspace to change values entered. Backspace to back up to prior steps and make changes.

**Q, q** Press Q to quit the program.
**Enter** Presses Enter to move on to the next step.
A short beep means the key pressed is inactive.

**Code 920 Add variables to *ADDview.h* and initialized variables to *OnInitialUpdate()* in *ADDview.cpp*.**

```
int m_nNew, m_nRepeat, m_nNewDigits, m_nQuit;
int m_npos, m_nslot, m_nmsg, m_ni, m_ntemp;
m_nNew = 0;
m_nRepeat = 0;
m_nNewDigits= 0;
m_nQuit = 0;
m_npos = 0;
m_nslot = 1;
m_nmsg = 0;
m_ni = 0;
m_nd1 = 1;
m_nd2 = 1;
```

# Programming with MFC

### Code 921 Add Code to *OnChar* in *ADDView.cpp* by hand

```cpp
void CADDView::OnChar(UINT nChar, UINT nRepCnt, UINT nFlags)
{
    // TODO: Add your message handler code here and/or call default
    int k;           // add to OnChar ADDView.cpp
    char buf[3];
    UINT ch;

    if(m_nStart==0)           //       B1
    {
        switch(nChar)
        {
        case VK_RETURN:      //Enter key
            m_nDigit ++;
            m_nChar = ' ';
            m_nCharYN = ' ';

            if (m_nNew == 1)
            {
                m_ni = 0;

                if (m_nd1 < m_nd2)
                {
                    m_ntemp = m_nd1;
                    m_nd1 = m_nd2;
                    m_nd2 = m_ntemp;

                    ch = m_nChar1;
                    m_nChar1 = m_nChar2;
                    m_nChar2 = ch;
                }

                seed();
                Numbers(m_nd1,m_nd2);

                for(k=0;k<WIDTH;k++) m_szN1[k]= '\0';
                _ltoa(m_ln1,m_szN1,10);

                for(k=0;k<WIDTH;k++) m_szN2[k]= '\0';
                _ltoa(m_ln2,m_szN2,10);

                for(k=0;k<WIDTH;k++) m_szResult[k]= '\0';
                for(k=0;k<m_nd1;k++) m_szResult[k]= ' ';

                for(k=0;k<WIDTH;k++) m_szCarry[k]= '\0';
                for(k=0;k<m_nd1;k++) m_szCarry[k]= ' ';

                for(k=0;k<WIDTH;k++) m_szLine[k]= '\0';
                for(k=0;k<m_nd1+1;k++) m_szLine[k]= '-';

                m_nStart = 1;
```

# 9 ADD

```
      m_nslot = 1;
      m_npos = 0;
    }
    m_nNew = 0;

    if (m_nRepeat == 1)
    {
      m_nDigit = 1;
      m_nChar1 = ' ';
      m_nChar2 = ' ';
    }
    m_nRepeat = 0;

    if (m_nDigit > 3)
    {
      m_nDigit = 1;
    }

    break;
case VK_BACK:    //Backspace key  0
    if (m_nDigit>1)
    {
      m_nDigit--;
      m_nChar =  ' ';
      m_nCharYN = ' ';
      m_nNew = 0;
    }
    else
    {
      MessageBeep((WORD) - 1);
    }
    break;
case 'Y':  //0
case 'y':
    if (m_nDigit<3) MessageBeep((WORD) - 1);

    if (m_nDigit>=3)
    {
      m_nCharYN = nChar;
      m_nNew = 1;
      m_nRepeat = 0;
    }
    break;
case 'N':  //0
case 'n':
    if (m_nDigit<3) MessageBeep((WORD) - 1);

    if (m_nDigit>=3)
    {
```

## Programming with MFC

```
            m_nCharYN = nChar;
            m_nRepeat = 1;   //start problem setup over
            m_nNew = 0;
          }
          break;

        case 'Q':
        case 'q'://quit 0
          exit(0);
          break;

        case '1':    //0
        case '2':    //0
        case '3':    //0
        case '4':    //0
        case '5':    //0
          if (m_nDigit==1)
          {
            m_nChar1 = nChar;
            buf[0] = (char) nChar;
            m_nd1 = atoi(buf);
          }

          if (m_nDigit==2)
          {
            m_nChar2 = nChar;
            buf[0] = (char) nChar;
            m_nd2 = atoi(buf);
          }
          break;

        default: //0  any other char do nothing
          MessageBeep((WORD) - 1);

      } //end of switch

      Invalidate(FALSE);   // redraw the screen

   } //end of m_nstart==0 if

// add code 923 here

} //end of OnChar
```

# 9 ADD

## 9.8 How the User Solves the Problem

The user solves the problem by entering digits 0 to 9 representing sum digits and 0, 1 carry digits in defined slots (Figures 905, 906). The user is guided by the caret that automatically moves from slot to slot in a predefined sequence. In this way the program shows the user how to actually do the addition as defined by the *Standard Addition Algorithm with Carry* (page 102).

**Figure 905 Sum and Carry Digits**
```
 0111   <--carries
 11979
+87957
------
 99936
```

**Figure 906 Slot Numbers**
```
 08642   < slot numbers
 11979
+87957
------
 197531  < slot numbers
```

**Problem display** Displaying the problem requires 5 strings and a + sign (Figure 905). The strings, actually char arrays, are for carries, number m_nd$_1$, number m_nd$_2$, a line under m_nd$_2$, and the result (the user's answer). A *TextOut* writes the + sign.

**Problem execution requires Screen Coordinates** The user enters digits into slots marked by a program controlled caret (cursor). We need screen coordinates for the slots.

Variables *m_nxChar* and *m_nyChar* define a rectangle representing the area a digit occupies (*SelectAFont,* Code 908 page 111).

The coordinates of the slot 1 rectangle (Figure 906) are the $x_0$, $y_0$ coordinates of the first character printed on the screen by the last code line that displays the problem on the screen.

The initial value of *m_nslot* is 1 and the initial value of *m_npos* is 0.

**x coordinate** The x coordinate of any column in the problem is
x = x0 + (*m_nd1* – *m_npos*)*m_nxChar*

*m_nd1* is the width of the number so that x = x0 + *m_nd*m_nxChar* is the position of the position 0 digit. Subtract *m_npos*m_nxChar* to move the caret to the left side of the character rectangle.

# Programming with MFC

**y coordinate** The y coordinate of the carry row in the problem is
y = y0 − m_nyChar+ 4*(m_nslot%2)*(m_nyChar)

The first *m_nyChar* puts the caret at the bottom of the rectangle. In a carry slot *m_nslot%2* = 1 so that 4*(m_nslot%2)*(m_nyChar) moves the caret into the current carry slot.

The users answer is stored in the string *m_szResult (see page 131 case 0 to 9 code)*
$$pDC \to TextOut(0,0,m\_szResult); \text{ (Code 913 p117)}.$$

The users answer is converted to a number in Code 923 on page 128
$$m\_lanswer = atol(m\_szResult);$$

**Code 922 Add m_nslot code after** // *add code 923* **to** *OnDraw* **in** *ADDView.cpp*

```
// number into current slot
if(m_nslot<=m_nmaxslot)
{
   pDC -> MoveTo(x0+(m_nd1 - m_npos)*m_nxChar,
                 y0-m_nyChar+(m_nslot%2)*4*m_nyChar);
   pDC->SetTextAlign(TA_UPDATECP | TA_RIGHT);
   pDC->TextOut(0,0,m_nChar);

   m_ptCaretPos = pDC -> GetCurrentPosition();
   m_ptCaretPos.y += m_nyChar;
   SetCaretPos(m_ptCaretPos);
}

// add code 924 here
```

### Relation of m_npos to m_nslot

| m_nslot | 1 | 2 | 3 | 4 | 5 | 6 | 7 |
|---|---|---|---|---|---|---|---|
| m_nslot%2 | 1 | 0 | 1 | 0 | 1 | 0 | 1 |
| m_nslot− (m_nslot%2) | 0 | 2 | 2 | 4 | 4 | 6 | 6 |
| m_npos | 0 | 1 | 1 | 2 | 2 | 3 | 3 |

Therefore m_npos = ½ [m_nslot − (m_nslot%2)]
m_nslot − (m_nslot%2)
**Maximum number of slots (carry + result)** The number of slots to be filled (*m_nmaxslot*) equals the number of sum digits *m_nd1* plus the number of carry digits *m_nd1* − 1, and *m_nmaxslot* = 2 *m_nd1* − 1

# 9 ADD

## 9.9 Processing Do-The-Problem Key Presses

Every key press generates a *WM_CHAR* message that calls the *OnChar* function, which includes two *switch* functions: one for problem setup and one for doing the problem. The *cases* in the *switch* functions define active keys.

The *WM_CHAR* messages created by inactive keys are discarded by the switch functions.

**Keys 0 to 9** Press a key in the range 0 to 9 as a sum digit in a slot or 0 to 1 as a carry digit in a slot.

User can type over digits (0 to 9) to change entries.

User does not have to enter the carries. Press Enter to skip over.

Nevertheless, if the user presses any sequence of keys (except Enter) only the numbers 0 to 9 will be printed. Pressing enter moves on to the next slot.

**Y, y**  Press the Y key to respond to the message.

**N, n**  Press the N key to respond to the message.

**Q, q**  Press the Q key to quit the program.

**Backspace** Before Enter is pressed the user can backspace to change sum digit or carry digit values. Backspace to back up to prior steps and make changes.

**Enter** Press Enter to move on to the next step.

A short beep means the key you pressed is inactive.

# Programming with MFC

## Code 923 Add code by hand to *OnChar* in *ADDView.cpp*

```
long m_lanswer;   // add to public ADDView.h

  else //start of m_nstart==1    //   B2
  {
    switch(nChar)
    {
      case VK_RETURN:   //Enter key  1
        // go to next slot
        m_nslot++;
        m_npos = (m_nslot - (m_nslot%2))/2;
        m_nChar = ' ';

        // is problem done?
        if ((m_ni==0) && (m_nslot==m_nmaxslot+1))
        {
          m_ni=1;  //problem done
          m_lanswer = atol(m_szResult);
        }

        // new problem with same number of digits
        if (m_nNew == 1)
        {
          Numbers(m_nd1,m_nd2);

          for(k=0;k<WIDTH;k++) m_szN1[k]= '\0';
          _ltoa(m_ln1,m_szN1,10);

          for(k=0;k<WIDTH;k++) m_szN2[k]= '\0';
          _ltoa(m_ln2,m_szN2,10);
        }
        m_nNew = 0;

        // repeat current problem
        if (m_nRepeat == 1)
        {
          m_ni=0;
          m_nslot = 1;
          m_npos = 0;

          for(k=0;k<WIDTH;k++) m_szResult[k]= '\0';
          for(k=0;k<m_nd1;k++) m_szResult[k]=' ';

          for(k=0;k<WIDTH;k++) m_szCarry[k]= '\0';
          for(k=0;k<m_nd1;k++) m_szCarry[k]=' ';
        }
        m_nRepeat = 0;

        // new problem with new numbers of digits
        if (m_nNewDigits==1)
```

```
    {
       m_nStart = 0;
       m_nDigit = 1;
       m_nslot = 1;
       m_npos = 0;
    }
    m_nNewDigits = 0;

    if (m_nQuit==1)
    {
       exit(0);
    }

    break;

case VK_BACK:    //Backspace key  1
   if ((m_ni==0) && (m_nslot>1))
   {
      m_nslot--;
      m_npos = (m_nslot - (m_nslot%2))/2;
      m_nChar = ' ';
   }
   else
   {
      MessageBeep((WORD) - 1);
   }
   break;

case 'Y':
case 'y': //   1
   if (m_ni==0) MessageBeep((WORD) - 1);

   switch(m_ni)
   {
   case 1:
      //not correct, try again
      if (m_lanswer != m_lresult)
      {
         m_nRepeat = 1;
      }

      //correct, do new problem
      if (m_lanswer == m_lresult)
      {
         m_nNew = 1;
         m_nRepeat = 1;
      }
      break;

   case 2:
      //not correct, do new problem
      if (m_lanswer!=m_lresult)
```

```
        {
          m_nNew = 1;
          m_nRepeat = 1;
        }
        break;

      case 3:
        // quit
        m_nQuit = 1;
        break;
    }
    break;

  case 'N':
  case 'n':   // 1
    //do nothing
    if (m_ni==0) MessageBeep((WORD) - 1);

    switch(m_ni)
    {
    case 1:
      //not correct,do not try again
      if (m_lanswer != m_lresult)
      {
        m_ni = 2;
        m_nNew = 0;
        m_nRepeat = 0;
        m_nNewDigits = 0;
      }

      //correct, do not do new problem
      if (m_lanswer == m_lresult)
      {
        m_ni = 3;
        m_nNew = 0;
        m_nRepeat = 0;
        m_nNewDigits = 0;
      }
      break;

    case 2:
      //not correct, do not do new problem
      if (m_lanswer!=m_lresult)
      {
        m_ni = 3;
        m_nNew = 0;
        m_nRepeat = 0;
        m_nNewDigits = 0;
      }
      break;
```

# 9 ADD

```
        case 3:

            // do new problem with new numbers of digits
            m_nNewDigits = 1;
            m_nQuit = 0;
            break;

        } //end of switch m_ni
        break;

    case 'Q':
    case 'q': //quit 1
        exit(0);
        break;

    case '0':   //1
    case '1':   //1
    case '2':   //1
    case '3':   //1
    case '4':   //1
    case '5':   //1
    case '6':   //1
    case '7':   //1
    case '8':   //1
    case '9':   //1
        if(m_ni==0)
        {
          m_nChar = nChar;
          if (m_nslot%2)
          {
             m_szResult[m_nd1 - m_npos] = (char) nChar;
          }
          else
          {
             m_szCarry[m_nd1 - m_npos] = (char) nChar;
          }
        }
        break;

    default:
        MessageBeep((WORD) - 1);
    } //end of switch else
    Invalidate();   // redraw the problem only

} //end of m_nstart==1 else

CView::OnChar(nChar, nRepCnt, nFlags);
} // end of OnChar
```

Programming with MFC

## 9.10 What-to-do-next Message Handlers

After a user completes a problem message boxes appear that offer the user choices equivalent to these.
"Your answer is correct - Do you want to do a new problem?"

"Your answer is not correct - Do you want to try it again, or do you want to do a new problem?"

"Do you want to quit. If no, then you can start over."

Every key press generates a *WM_CHAR* message that calls the *OnChar* function, which invokes a switch function. Key press responses are implemented by switch function cases.

**Code 924 Add Switch code to *OnDraw* in *ADDView.cpp***

```
// display and do the problem
switch(m_ni)   //process message box responses
{
case 1:
  // correct/not correct
  if (m_lanswer == m_lresult)
  {
    m_nmsg=AfxMessageBox("Correct! DO A NEW PROBLEM?",MB_YESNO,0);

    switch (m_nmsg)
    {
      case IDYES:
        SendMessage(WM_CHAR,'y',0);
        SendMessage(WM_CHAR,VK_RETURN,0);
        break;

      case IDNO:
        SendMessage(WM_CHAR,'n',0);
        SendMessage(WM_CHAR,VK_RETURN,0);
        break;
    }
  }
  else
  {
    m_nmsg=AfxMessageBox("Not correct. TRY IT AGAIN?",MB_YESNO,0);
```

# 9 ADD

```
    switch (m_nmsg)
    {
      case IDYES:
        SendMessage(WM_CHAR,'y',0);
        SendMessage(WM_CHAR,VK_RETURN,0);
        break;

      case IDNO:
        SendMessage(WM_CHAR,'n',0);
        SendMessage(WM_CHAR,VK_RETURN,0);
        break;
    }
  }
  break;

case 2:
  //do a new problem if not correct?
  m_nmsg=AfxMessageBox("DO A NEW PROBLEM?",MB_YESNO,0);
  switch (m_nmsg)
  {
    case IDYES:
      SendMessage(WM_CHAR,'y',0);
      SendMessage(WM_CHAR,VK_RETURN,0);
      break;
    case IDNO:
      SendMessage(WM_CHAR,'n',0);
      SendMessage(WM_CHAR,VK_RETURN,0);
      break;
  }
  break;

case 3:
  //Change number of digits or quit
  m_nmsg=AfxMessageBox("QUIT? (on No you start over)",MB_YESNO,0);

  switch (m_nmsg)
  {
    case IDYES:
      SendMessage(WM_CHAR,'y',0);
      SendMessage(WM_CHAR,VK_RETURN,0);
      break;
    case IDNO:
      SendMessage(WM_CHAR,'n',0);
      SendMessage(WM_CHAR,VK_RETURN,0);
      break;
  }

} //end of m_ni switch
```

Programming with MFC

## 9.11 A Simple Help Function

This is the simple help system. A right mouse click accesses it (JP102).

**This is for a mouse action**
Click on *View*, click on *Class Wizard*, click on *Message Maps*.
Verify Project is *ADD*, Class name is *CADDView*.
In the *Object Ids* box click on *ADDView*
In the *Messages* box click on *WM_RButtonDown*.
Click on *Add Function* to add *OnRButtonDown*
Click on *Edit Code* to see function added as a skeleton message handler.
Add following code to the message handler.

**Code 925 Add OnRButtonDown to *ADDView.cpp*.**

```
void CADDView::OnRButtonDown(UINT nFlags, CPoint point)
{
    // TODO: Add your message handler code here and/or call default
    CString strRightClick ;

    strRightClick = (CString)
        "Use keyboard to enter numbers; press Enter to continue."
        + "\n\n"
        + "The maximum number of digits is 5"
        + "\n"
        + "Can quit anytime (use keys: q,Q)"
        + "\n"
        + "Can type over numbers (0 to 9) to change your entries."
        + "\n"
        + "You do not have to enter the carries. Press Enter to skip over."
        + "\n"
        + "Press Enter to proceed to the next step."
        + "\n"
        + "Press Backspace to back up to prior step and make changes."
        + "\n"
        + "Respond to requests with yes or no (use keys: y,Y,n,N)"
        + "\n"
        + "A short beep means the key you pressed is inactive";

    MessageBox(strRightClick, "Active Keys: Enter, Backspace, q, Q, y, Y, n, N, 0 to 9", MB_OK);

    CView::OnRButtonDown(nFlags, point);
}
```

## 9.12 Variable Definitions and Initial Values

Here are all of the variables and prototypes used in the *ADD* program. DO NOT add to *ADDView.h*. **This is a recapitulation.**

**Code 927 Variable and Prototype Definitions added to *ADDView.h***

```
#define WIDTH 8
// Overrides  (added in Section 2.1)
public:
virtual void OnDraw(CDC* pDC);  // overridden to draw this view   //nlp
virtual void OnInitialUpdate();

// Generated message map functions
protected:
  //{{AFX_MSG(CAddView)   //nlp
  afx_msg void OnChar(UINT nChar, UINT nRepCnt, UINT nFlags);
  afx_msg void OnKillFocus(CWnd* pNewWnd);
  afx_msg void OnRButtonDown(UINT nFlags, CPoint point);
  afx_msg void OnSetFocus(CWnd* pOldWnd);
  //}}AFX_MSG

private:
  UINTm_nChar1, m_nChar2, m_nChar, m_nCharYN;
  CPoint m_ptCaretPos;
  int m_nxChar, m_nyChar;

public:
  void seed();
  void SelectAFont(int n,CDC* pDC);
  long RandRange(long min, long max);
  void Numbers(int nd1, int nd2);

  long m_lmx1, m_lmx2;   //10^nd1, 10^nd2
  long m_ln1, m_ln2;   // N1, N2
  long m_lresult,m_lanswer;

  int m_nd1,m_nd2;      // number of digits in N1,N2
  int m_nStart,m_nDigit,m_ntemp;
  int m_npos,m_nslot,m_nmaxslot;
  int m_nmsg, m_ni;
  int m_nNew, m_nRepeat, m_nNewDigits, m_nQuit;
  char m_szResult[WIDTH];
  char m_szCarry[WIDTH];
  char m_szLine[WIDTH];
  char m_szN1[WIDTH];
  char m_szN2[WIDTH];
  CFont* m_pOldFont;
```

Programming with MFC

# Index

#define ........................................... 20
? Operator ........................................ 90

ADD – add two integers ............. 101
    Addition algorithm ............ 102
    Caret and the Font ............. 109
    Creating numbers to add ... 118
    Displaying the problem ..... 116
    Events drive the problem .. 103
    Help .................................... 134
    OnDraw and OnChar ........ 107
    Processing Setup keys ....... 121
    Processing Do keys ........... 127
    Project Design .................... 105
    Setting up the problem ...... 112
    User solves the problem .... 125
    Variables & Initial Values . 135
    What to do next ................. 132

Add a Push Button ....................... 16
Add Push Button Handlers .......... 18
Add Code to Message Handler .. 20
Array ............................................ 88

Build and Execute a project ......... 4

Change Dialog Size        12,.. .46
char  ............................................ 23
Create a project ............................. 1
CString .......................................... 22

Dialog based project ..................... 3
Document & View project ............ 1
Drawing in a Window .................. 7

GetLength( ) ................................ 22

Hello World .................................. 6
How Visual C++ Works .............. 1
How to Position a Control .......... 14
If-Else ........................................... 21

Multiple Document View ............ 3

Oscilloscope ................................ 45
    Add push button ................ 49
    Add message handler ........ 50
    Add Static controls ............ 53
    Change Dialog Size ........... 46
    Combo box ......................... 54
    Combo & Slider Variables . 63
    CrtScreen ............................ 65
    Front Panel Design ............. 47
    Help ..................................... 66
    Slider .................................. 58

Position a Control ....................... 14
Property Sheet - Menu ................. 67
    Add Controls to pages ........ 71
    Apply .................................. 78
    Connect to Menu ................ 76
    Project Design .................... 67
    Property Pages ................... 68
    Property Sheet .................... 70
    Rectangle – display ........... 79
    Wizard ................................ 79

Signal Generator ......................... 11
    Add push button ................ 16
    Change Dialog Size ........... 12
    Frequency ........................... 27
    Front Panel Design ............ 13
    Help .................................... 42
    How to Position a Control.. 14
    Keypad and code ............... 16
    OnPaint .............................. 26
    Pulse ................................... 39
    Sine ..................................... 38
    Triangle .............................. 40
    Variables ............................ 25
    Waveform .......................... 32
    WaveformScreen ............... 41

Single Document View ................ 1

Sliders, more about .................... 80
    Adding controls ................. 82
    Project Design .................... 81
    Project ................................ 81

# Index

Tic Tac Toe............................... 85
    Data fetching ..................... 92
    Document functions .......... 86
    Help ................................. 100
    Menu items........................ 98
    OnNewDocument( )........... 91
    Project Design ................... 85
    View functions ................. 92
    Mouse buttons code ........... 96

Writing the Window's Title........ 5

Made in the USA
Middletown, DE
15 December 2022

18641881R00086